Withdrawn

A Thousand
Miles to Freedom

A Thousand Miles to Freedom

❧

My Escape from North Korea

EUNSUN KIM
WITH SÉBASTIEN FALLETTI

Translated by David Tian

St. Martin's Press New York

www.stmartins.com

Designed by Kathryn Parise

The Library of Congress Cataloging-in-Publication Data is available upon request.

ISBN 978-1-250-06464-6 (hardcover)
ISBN 978-1-4668-7088-8 (e-book)

St. Martin's Press books may be purchased for educational, business, or
promotional use. For information on bulk purchases, please contact the
Macmillan Corporate and Premium Sales Department at 1-800-221-7945,
extension 5442, or write to specialmarkets@macmillan.com.

First published in France in 2012 by Éditions Michel Lafon under the title
Corée du Nord—9 ans pour fuir l'enfer.

First U.S. Edition: July 2015

10 9 8 7 6 5 4 3 2 1

For the youth of North Korea:
That you may find
freedom and the right to dream

Acknowledgments

❖

My heartfelt thanks to Soojin Park, Eunji Park, and Jiwon Lim, who helped translate my thoughts and who gave immeasurably to this project.

Everything recounted in this book is true. However, to protect the members of my family who still remain in North Korea, I am writing under a pseudonym, and other names and details have been changed.

A Thousand
Miles to Freedom

❊ 1

December 1997

For nearly a week, I had been alone in our tiny, freezing apartment in Eundeok, the town in North Korea where I was born. Other than a coffee table and a wooden dresser, my parents had sold all of our furniture to buy food to fill our stomachs. Even the carpeting was gone, so I slept on the cement floor in a makeshift sleeping bag pulled together from old clothes. The walls were completely bare except for two framed, side-by-side portraits of our "Eternal President" Kim Il-sung and his successor, the "Dear Leader" Kim Jong-il, staring down at me. Selling these portraits would have been considered sacrilege, punishable by death.

Even though darkness was starting to fall on this late December afternoon, I could still just manage to read what

I was writing. Once the sun went down, I would have no more light—electricity no longer worked in the apartment, and besides, the lightbulbs had been gone for quite some time already. There was no more heating, either, but I hardly felt the cold at all, because I was completely exhausted after several days without eating. I was sure that I was about to die of hunger.

And so I started to write my last will and testament.

I was eleven years old.

Earlier that Day

For the third time in the past week, I decided to go out in search of my mother and Keumsun, my older sister. They had left our apartment six days ago for Rajin-Sonbong, a large city nearby, to try to find food, since there was nothing left to eat in Eundeok. Mustering up all the courage I had within me, I crossed the bridge over the river and took the main road up to the train station. There were not many people walking along the sidewalks, but even so I made sure to get a good look at everyone who passed by, just in case my mother was coming back from the other direction. On my left, I glimpsed the noodle shop where I used to love eating, where my dad had taken me on special occasions. A little farther up the road, I caught sight of the photo studio where my family had once had a family portrait taken. When I finally reached the bus station, I was given permission to ride for free in the back of a crowded shuttle bus on the way to Rajin-Sonbong, a trip that takes about an hour. I was probably allowed on for free because I was still a child.

Throughout the entire trip, in my desperation to find my mother, I nervously scrutinized every car and every truck we passed along the way. My efforts were in vain; at the terminal, I found myself alone amid a barrage of uniformed men. In front of me, an electric fence protected the entrance to Rajin-Sonbong. A special permit was required to enter the city. I must have waited at the gate for a good hour or so, hopefully and anxiously watching everyone who walked out, searching for my mother's face. Unfortunately, neither my mom nor Keumsun emerged from the crowd. At last, disheartened, I decided to return home, since nightfall was rapidly approaching.

I had made the same journey twice before, but after this trip, I was sure the two of them would never come back to me. Something must have happened to them. Or maybe, it occurred to me, they had decided to abandon me. With a heavy, bitter heart, I began to resent my mother. As she was leaving, she had told me she would bring back something to eat "in two or three days." She left me fifteen North Korean won to live on, which, at the time, seemed like quite a large fortune in my eyes. I was thrilled at first—I'd never had so much money before in my life. My eyes shone brightly with excitement. Like a real adult, I proudly went by myself to the *jangmadang*, the market next to the river. At the market, I bought a block of tofu, and then I returned to our little apartment on the second floor of our building. There, I ate the flabby tofu by the spoonful, rationing it so that it would last until my family returned. For two days, I stayed at home, watching people on the street through the window. Ever since my father had died a few weeks earlier, on November 11, my sister and I no longer attended school. We were too busy looking for the roots and timber in the mountains which we needed to eat or sell to survive. Besides, we would have been embarrassed to go back to school, since we no longer had any presentable clothes. We had sold everything we had and were wearing rags. When I went outside these days, I was always afraid of running into classmates.

❖

After forty-eight hours had passed, hunger began to gnaw at my stomach, and my fear of being abandoned started to swell. When I finished eating the tofu, there was nothing else left in the apartment to eat. And my mom had still not returned home yet. I lay down and tried to sleep on the floor, closing my eyes and counting to ten in my head;

surely, she would come back by the time I finished. But when I got to ten, nothing happened, so then I counted in reverse from ten to one. Still, nothing changed.

Soon, I started skipping meals. On the balcony, I found some dusty turnip leaves, left over from when we had spread them there to dry in the sun. I grabbed some of the least discolored leaves to boil and make into a soup. For two days, I survived on this tasteless concoction.

Another two days passed, during which time I didn't eat anything. Except for my third trip to Rajin-Sonbong, I no longer even had enough energy to go out and beg or steal. Little by little, my body started to get used to the stabbing hunger in my stomach, but I lost all of my strength. Overcome by my weakness, I tried to sleep. I felt like the ground was going to open up and swallow me, like I was going to get sucked into the depths of the earth.

Suddenly, I realized I was going to die soon. This was it. By the time my family came back, it would be too late. Ever since the start of the Arduous March—the great North Korean famine of the mid-1990s—I had known I wasn't going to make it through alive. I had become so used to the idea that I wasn't even afraid of dying anymore. Even so, I knew that I didn't want to leave the world like this, without a trace of myself left behind. At once, I decided to write my testament. I wanted to tell my mom all that I had gone through. I wanted to let her know that I had waited for her, that I had tried my best to find her. And, especially, I wanted her to know that I felt abandoned.

In the drawer of the coffee table, I fished out a small notebook and a pencil from among the few valuable items that we had not sold. The paper in the notebook was of good quality. Crouched under the twilight, I started to write my will. In the notebook, I recounted all my trials and tribulations, as well as my three voyages to and from Rajin-Sonbong. Clenching my pencil tightly, and full of despair, I filled out an entire page.

Mom, *I wrote.* I am waiting for you. I have been waiting for you for six days. I feel like I'm going to die soon. Why haven't you come back to me yet?

After finishing the page, I started crying and fell to the ground as the darkness of night gradually began to envelop me. Suddenly, I heard noise coming from the stairs. My heart started to skip.

Alas, it was just the neighbors, returning home to their apartment.

I left my will on the coffee table and, my face soaked in tears, I laid myself down and closed my eyes. I was sure that I was never going to wake up again.

※ 2

March 2011

The automated doors slam shut. The train I'm taking rattles back and forth as it passes through the
underground tunnels of Seoul's subway system. As I lean
against the glass window, a medley of bright colors from
advertisements starts to appear on the dark walls of the
tunnel, with slogans that I can't seem to make out. Everything here in Seoul, South Korea, moves so quickly, including the metro.

My name is Eunsun Kim and today, as I write this, I am
twenty-five years old.

If you were to look at me, you would probably assume I
was just like any other college student. Because of my slight
figure, you might not even realize that I am older than all
of my friends. In about forty minutes, I will arrive at the

entrance of Sogang University, one of the best universities in South Korea. My campus is not as impressive as those of the prestigious Korea University or Yonsei University, but regardless, I feel right at home there, with its familiar landmarks and the many friends I have made.

I have my day already planned out. Equipped with my black-and-orange Samsung laptop, I am planning to spend the day preparing for my exams in the library. With my iPhone in its purple case, I text my friends and arrange a quick meet-up at the Starbucks on campus. I like the caffe latte—the espresso is a bit bitter for my taste. After getting my coffee, I'll go back to the library, where I will try not to fall asleep while reading my textbooks. At Sogang University, I study Chinese language and culture, and later you will understand what led me to these subjects.

In South Korea, the competition to get the best grades is fierce, but still, I try my best. Few of my classmates are even aware that I did not have the opportunity to go to school for many years, and for the most part, I try to maintain a low profile to avoid drawing attention to the delay in my education. I enjoy learning and studying, especially at the beginning of each semester when the professors are fresh and enthusiastic. Later tonight, around ten o'clock, I'll return to our little apartment, situated right in the heart of Seoul, where I'll see my older sister, Keumsun, and my mother.

❖

Seoul, the capital city of South Korea, is a true metropolis, with over fifteen million residents, a skyline covered with tall skyscrapers, and an extensive highway system. The mighty Han River flows through the middle of the city, but in winter, when the river is frozen, you can just walk directly across the river without using any of the bridges. Behind the river stand several steep mountains, and at the summit of one of them sits an immense tower built for television broadcasts. The Namsan Tower is the symbol of Seoul, the city that took me in, the city that I now call home. Here, traffic jams sometimes last for hours on end, even during heavy July rains, and the rent for apartments is sky-high. But life here is also so exhilarating, so convenient, and everything moves so fast. High-speed Internet is available everywhere. There is something interesting and fun to do on every street corner, both day and night.

I often meet up with my friends in Sinchon, a student neighborhood, to drink *maekju*, a local beer, in the bars that never seem to close. In the bars we also eat dried octopus and grilled *jjukkumi*, a "baby" species with five arms each—a real treat. They are small enough that you can swallow them in just one bite. My friends refuse to believe me when I tell them seafood is fresher and tastier in North Korea. But it's true! They don't always understand me, because I come from a different world entirely. And most people could never even begin to imagine this other world where I was born and raised.

❖

The high-speed train vibrates below my feet. All around me, *ajumas*—the Korean term used to address married or middle-age women—watch their favorite shows on their cell phones with antennas sticking out. Some students, perched atop their high heels and holding on to the train's metal bars for balance, are listening to their iPods. Others, staring into their pocket mirrors, are applying mascara. They disdainfully ignore the street vendor trying to sell his Frank Sinatra CDs. Talking through speakers on wheels that he drags along behind him, the vendor tries to peddle his CD collection to the older gentlemen on the train. As the train travels from station to station, the platforms fill up and empty almost mechanically.

The silence of the South Korean metro allows me to ruminate for a moment. I begin reflecting on my memories of the train stations in Pyongyang, the capital of North Korea, that I visited with my dad such a long time ago. The stations were so magnificent and luxurious, with big beautiful purple chandeliers, like something you might expect to see in a major Hollywood film. The train stations in Seoul are much blander. I will remember the trip we made to

Pyongyang for the rest of my life. I was nine years old, and we were by ourselves, Keumsun, my father, and me. Mom didn't come with us; she preferred to stay back home and take care of things at the apartment. Even though the famine was already taking hold and we had nothing to eat, the trip to Pyongyang felt magical. There weren't any skyscrapers in sight, but we saw a hotel under construction that reached a hundred and fifty meters in height. Workers and machines dangled from the top of the hotel. From such a distance, they appeared so tiny that they looked like little ants.

❖

Only three stations now separate me from the Sogang University campus, and my heart starts beating faster and faster as the train accelerates. The speed of the train makes me feel a certain melancholy in my heart: it reminds me that I am from a completely different world. Where I'm from, it took two long days to get from Eundeok, the little town where we lived, to Chongjin, just ninety-five kilometers away, where my grandparents lived. The trip to Chongjin was always an exhausting one. We would pass through frigid temperatures, and we were always crammed together in the train like farm animals. We relieved ourselves of bodily waste using little tins we carried with us. If we moved, we would lose our spot to someone else. In South Korea, I can travel the same distance in under twenty minutes on a high-speed train. Back in North Korea, only the capital had modern amenities, like the metro stations that I found so dazzling.

I now find myself thinking of everyone I left behind, all of the people from whom I have heard nothing at all since I left my country. Then I was eleven years old, hungry, and without a home. My aunts, my uncles, my friends at school … have they survived the famine? On the train, another rider stares at me out of the corner of his eye, as if I am some outsider who doesn't belong here. Still, I have tried my hardest to blend in, with my high heels, short skirt, and tight jacket. Whether or not I have succeeded in looking like I'm from South Korea, the reality is that I was born in Eundeok, a small industrial village in North Hamgyong Province, on August 15, 1986, in North Korea. In my quest for liberty and freedom, I have finally reached South Korea, after a nine-year journey across China and Mongolia. Here in Seoul, I have a passport. I no longer have to live in hiding, and I have built a new life for myself.

However, my memories of the north regularly come back to me, and one question in particular still haunts me: Why must the people of my home country continue to live in such suffering? Since arriving in Seoul, I have learned, through reading various books and newspapers, that the misery in North Korea is the fault of an absurd totalitarian regime. The country is a complete economic disaster. The Kim family dynasty, the world's only communist dynasty, ruthlessly crushes any dissent.

These answers do not satisfy me and do little to assuage the unease in my heart. On the contrary, in fact, these answers make me feel totally powerless. I live barely forty kilometers from the barbed-wire border that separates me from my homeland, and yet there is nothing that I can do for my people, who are drained of energy by the famine and by the repression of an unrelenting totalitarian regime. For the twenty-five million people who live there, North Korea has become a true hell on earth, forgotten by the rest of the world. Even South Koreans, who share the same blood heritage, seem to have forgotten about the plight of their northern counterparts. At times, I feel overwhelmed by this sense of helplessness, by the feeling that there is nothing I can do to help my brothers and sisters to the north.

❖

"Sinchon Station."

The robotic voice coming from the loudspeakers breaks the silence of the train and pulls me away from my thoughts. I get off the train and start walking up the stairs in my usual automaton-like manner. This time, however, as soon as I step back aboveground, I decide that I will no longer sit back and do nothing. I have to tell my story to the world.

I have to tell my story to give a voice to the millions of North Koreans who are dying slowly and in silence. And I have to tell the world about the hundreds of thousands among them who have tried to escape from that hellhole, who are presently in hiding in China, fearing for their lives. Here I am, twenty-two miles deep into the promised land of South Korea. And yet here, refugees from the north are still treated as second-class citizens, when the only sin we are guilty of is refusing to die from starvation.

Because my North Korean brothers and sisters do not have the ability to speak out for themselves, I am writing on their behalf. One day, I am sure, the two Koreas will reunite. It will be a long, complicated process, but it *will* happen. For the Korean peninsula to reunite, we are going to need the help of the entire world. But in order to find the solution, we first must understand the roots of the problem.

Since that fateful day in December when I was eleven years old, the day I wrote my will, I have, along with my mother and my sister, found some of these roots.

This is my story.

As a young girl, I never could have imagined that my life would change so quickly and so drastically. I didn't know it then, but after the winter of 1997, I would no longer have my childhood. For many years, up until I was nine years old, I was a very happy little girl. I had everything I could possibly want in life.

❖

Eundeok, my hometown, was located on the northeastern tip of the mountainous country of North Korea, fewer than fifteen kilometers away from the Tumen River, which separated the country from China and Russia. On the other side of the river, it took less than one hour to get to the sea. During the winter it was bitterly cold, and the snow stayed for weeks on end under an immense blue sky. Sometimes, I had to go to school trudging through a thick fog of white. My birthday, on the other hand, was in the middle of summer and was always warm and humid. It was on the same date that we celebrated the day Korea was liberated from Japanese rule in 1945. My birthday was always a very happy time.

Although it was surrounded by factories, my hometown was not very large. In just one hour, you could tour the entire town. On the horizon, you could make out a few trees on the mountains far away, but the nearby hills were all stripped bare, because the forests had been razed for firewood. Before reaching the first few buildings in town, you would find several mines that had become famous; many former, now disgraced, leaders from Pyongyang had been sent to work in them as punishment. The army also had several bases nearby, just like they do everywhere else in the country. We lived in perpetual fear of an invasion from the United States or from their ally, South Korea. Whenever I climbed the mountains to collect mushrooms, I caught sight of some large cannons, more or less hidden in the landscape. A little farther up, there were some barracks that we tried to avoid, because the men in the army had a bad reputation. They often abused their power to take advantage of poor people or those less fortunate. If a group of soldiers ran into a man smoking a cigarette, for instance, they could ask him to hand over his pack of cigarettes. If the man said no, the soldiers would make sure he learned to never refuse them again.

In the middle of Eundeok flows a river, with a large bridge linking either side. I sometimes liked to wade in that river, from which I lived ten minutes away by foot. The biggest buildings in the city, all made of gray cement, with balconies painted white or pink, had at most five floors. There were no advertisements anywhere. All of the walls there were either bare or plastered with propaganda praising our "Dear Leader" Kim Jong-il and the "socialist paradise" he had created for us in North Korea. The building in which I lived was only three floors, with heavily cracked walls.

"This building is bound to collapse," all the neighbors used to say.

In spite of everything, for the first few years of the 1990s, I generally felt pretty content. Nothing made me happier than to have my father pick me up after school. Some days, he would take me to the movies, using tickets he had gotten ahold of as a result of his connections at work. He worked at a weapons factory called "January 20th," named in commemoration of the day that Kim Il-sung, the founder of North Korea, paid it a personal visit. In North Korea, the names of most buildings were dates, in honor of visits from North Korean leaders. This policy of naming things after dates was one of the practices meant to maintain the cult of propaganda surrounding our heads of state, but it was only much later that I understood this.

Every time we went to the movies, my dad would meet me in front of the theater during the afternoon. I walked to the theater all by myself, like I was a real adult. But it was not enough to simply have a ticket. The hardest part was finding a seat, because people always rushed to get into the theater. So my dad would mount me up high upon his shoulders as we made our way through the crowd. Going to the movies and sitting on my dad's shoulders in the darkened theater were some of the happiest moments of my life. We watched films about brave heroes fighting against the imperialist Japanese colonizers. All around the screen, there were inscriptions that read, "Let us all unite behind the great general Kim Jong-il!"

Sometimes, my dad would also take me to street vendors to buy some *naengmyeon*, "cold noodles," a North Korean specialty from Pyongyang. We would bring a bowl, and my dad would proudly present the young lady working there with food coupons given to him by the government. After receiving the noodles, we would take them home to eat. I had never tasted anything so delicious. Even if there wasn't quite enough to satisfy our hunger, that couldn't ruin the happiness I felt at being able to eat these noodles.

In those years, my parents would never have been able to imagine that they would soon be dying of hunger, because they came from "good" families. That is to say, their families were part of the elite class; they had connections in the army and in the Workers' Party, which ruled North Korea. When my parents were very young, they both lived in Pyongyang, a privileged city reserved only for the elite. My grandfather was a highly ranked officer who dreamed of one day sending my mother to Kim Il-sung University, the most prestigious university in our country and the school where Kim Jong-il himself had studied. To ensure my mom could get the good grades necessary for admission, her father bribed the teachers by renovating the playground. Unfortunately for him, my mom was a tomboy who didn't really care much for school—she wanted to become a driver. What's more, on the day of the big university-entrance exam, she arrived late. And just like that, my grandfather's ambitious plans for my mother collapsed.

Since then, however, my mother has proven herself to be a person of remarkably strong character, a trait which, without a doubt, saved my life. She was essentially the head of our house. She's not very imposing in size, but she is highly intelligent and very determined. Even when she falls ill, her face still looks healthy and strong and doesn't show anything out of the ordinary. In this respect, I am a lot like my mother. When I was little, any time I was feeling sick, I could never get anyone to believe me because I still appeared healthy, and I was always sent off to school anyway. Maybe it was this ability that allowed me to survive while others did not.

In Eundeok, it was my mother who, thanks to her job working at the hospital, provided the household with food. Whatever food we needed she brought from the cafeteria at work, which kept us from going hungry for many years. She often complained about my father and his lack of common sense. She found him to be both too naïve and not physically strong enough. I remember looking at their wedding photo and thinking that he looked fairly robust, but then I would have to remind myself again that in reality, he had indeed become quite frail. Once, my mother sent him out to steal corn from the cornfields, so that we could have something to eat. Not only did he come back empty-handed, but he was also missing his coat. He must have given it to the farmers who caught him in the act and threatened to denounce him to the regime. Mom was *furious*. In Korea, if a man wants a woman to respect him, he needs to be strong. Their marriage was arranged by my maternal grandmother as my mom was leaving Pyongyang for Chongjin, the large port city on the eastern shore of North Korea.

My dad had no business sense, but there was one thing he was passionate about: writing. At the factory, it was always he who volunteered to write reports and propaganda.

Above all, he had a heart of gold, and as his daughter, that was good enough for me.

I could also always count on my older sister, Keumsun, to protect me whenever I felt trouble coming my way. If boys ever came to bother me, she didn't hesitate to confront them. Although we were once mistaken for twins, I don't think Keumsun and I look very much alike. She is two years older than I am, but she is smaller, with darker skin, and large eyes that contrast with mine. On the other hand, we have the same nose, and you can definitely tell that we belong to the same family. More than anything, Keumsun has always had this dynamic personality; she is confident in herself, and can persuade just about anyone that she is right. In Eundeok, my parents' friends nicknamed her the "Little Adult" because of how grown-up she seemed.

❖

As a child, I enjoyed going to school and I was a good student. Every morning it was the same routine. While it was still dark out, Mom would wake us up. Then I washed my face with cold water, which in winter was often freezing. After cleaning myself up, I carefully ironed my school uniform, which consisted of a navy blue skirt, a white blouse, and a little red scarf that signified membership in the Children's League. I was not yet allowed to wear the little pin with Kim Jong-il's likeness on it that everyone pinned over his or her breast after joining the Youth League.

While it was still not yet light outside, I would rush out to find my friends in the big esplanade at the center of town. At seven o'clock sharp, we marched to school row by row, class by class, all while singing songs in praise of our country's leaders:

"Even though we are small, our spirit is large! We are always ready to serve the great general Kim Jong-il!"

One of my favorite songs was called "A Thousand Miles of Learning." The lyrics recounted the young Kim Il-sung's odyssey across mountains in China while he was fighting the Japanese imperialists.

After ten minutes of military-style marching, my classmates and I would stop all at once and the teachers would come to inspect our uniforms. Finally, once we passed inspection, we were allowed in the classroom. We started every day with a silent reading, generally a page about Kim Jong-il's youth, from which we had to draw lessons about how to behave ourselves. One time, we read a story about Kim Jong-suk, Kim Jong-il's mother, who was gathering grains in front of the intrigued eyes of her son.

"Why are you doing that, Mommy? We have enough to eat already," asked the future dictator of our country.

"Because not a single one of our country's precious resources should go to waste," responded his mother wisely.

I didn't always understand the hidden message in each of these anecdotes, but I tried to commit them to memory anyway, because the teachers asked us to do so.

In class, I often looked around furtively. There were forty of us, sitting at tables aligned neatly along the floor.

The teacher's large wooden desk sat atop the platform at the front of the classroom. On the wall behind it hung a blackboard and, above that, there was a portrait of Kim Jong-il, carefully watching us at all times. At the back of the room, there was a stove, which we used in winter to heat up our lunches.

Every morning when the teacher entered the room, she selected one of us to read the page about Kim Jong-il out loud. Studying the lives of our country's leaders was one of the most important subjects we had at school, along with mathematics, Korean language arts, and the communist ethic.

We were expected to sit in class silently. Even the tiniest bit of disturbance was met with public humiliation: in front of the whole class, the teacher would beat us with her pointer stick. At the time, I thought it was only fair that these troublemakers should be punished in this way. However, I should add that I never received this kind of treatment myself, because I was considered a good student.

Nevertheless, my status as a good student did not excuse me from the self-criticism sessions that were mandatory for everyone in the country, whether you were a factory worker or a student. In my classroom, at the end of each day, each person had to confess his or her misdeeds in front of the entire class. I remember one day I made a critical remark while toiling in the teacher's garden, a task assigned to the "good students."

"What's the point of gathering all this corn if we won't be able to eat it?" I grumbled to myself.

"That individualistic attitude is unacceptable in the socialist society of North Korea!" my teacher sharply rebuked me, when she called me over after a classmate denounced me.

The next day, I reluctantly had to do my self-criticism. As soon as I finished, as payback I denounced the behavior of the classmate who had sold me out. To be honest, I felt a sense of sadistic pleasure in getting revenge because I was jealous of this girl. Her dad worked in the same factory as mine, but since he was ranked one level higher than my father, her family received better provisions than mine did.

At school, you needed to respect the class hierarchy. At the beginning of each year, we "elected" a class president and other people responsible for other important tasks. Even though officially these were free elections, there was only ever one candidate for each position. It's only now, as I reflect back on my childhood, that I realize the elections were just for show.

Here's an example of how the elections went: Once, the day before the election, the teacher called me over privately, probably because I was a good student. The next day, she asked the class:

"Do any of you have a candidate in mind?"

The room was silent. After a few moments had passed, I nervously lifted my finger and pointed at one of the students:

"Kim Song-ku," I said, following the orders I had been given the night beforehand.

"Do we all agree?" the teacher asked the class.

Without hesitating, the class unanimously approved, and this is how my friend Kim Song-ku was elected. His father was a carpenter, and we suspected that his father was supplying the teacher with firewood. In North Korea, the best way to ensure the success of one's children in school was to offer gifts to the teachers. This was something that my parents never seemed to understand.

One time during the elections, however, I received quite the surprise. The teacher asked the students to elect someone to be responsible for cleaning up the classroom after class each day. It wasn't the most glamorous of jobs, but it conferred a certain status of prestige in the school. A boy stood up and announced my name. My cheeks turned bright red as soon as he said my name. At that age, I was still very shy around boys and didn't really talk to any. I'd never really noticed this boy before, but after that day, I developed a secret crush on him. His badge had two stripes and three stars, which was considered a very high honor. I had only two stars. These emblems designated the hierarchy of the class, the best of whom had three stripes and three stars. The teacher awarded these stripes and stars to reward the best students, the ones who were smartest, or those who volunteered for a class duty. She also often rewarded those children whose parents were generous toward her or toward the school. For example, once when a window broke, a boy's parents offered to pay for its repair. Just like that, their son was promoted in the class hierarchy. This was how things happened in North Korea. Unfortunately for Keumsun and me, my parents never fully understood how this system worked.

For a long time after I was nominated to clean the classroom, I wondered if the boy who had nominated me had done so because he liked me or because he had been told to do so by the teacher. To this day, I still do not know.

I don't know what's become of him, and I will probably never find out.

❖ 4

I will remember one fateful afternoon in July 1994 in vivid detail for the rest of my life.

I was nearly eight years old. It was pouring rain outside. At the time, we were living in a small house, and the rain was pounding down so hard that the roof was leaking. With my dad, I was running from one end of the room to the other trying to arrange buckets to collect the rain and avoid flooding in the house. Suddenly, we heard a loud knock at the front door. When we opened the door, we found a man who looked quite bewildered standing on our porch, dripping wet. It was the head of our neighborhood, known as the *inminbanjang*. Just the mention of his name struck fear throughout the neighborhood, because he was in charge of monitoring and reporting to the authorities everything that happened on our block.

The entire country was littered with these worrisome people, who even to this day ensure that the regime maintains its iron grip over the lives of twenty-five million North Koreans.

"Make sure you watch the news tonight," the *inminbanjang* ordered us, and he seemed as confused as we were. There must have been something important planned for the broadcast that night.

Then, as quickly as the man had arrived, he disappeared again through the pouring rain. It was the first time we had ever received this kind of directive from him.

❖

When the news came on that night, I sat in front of the television next to Keumsun and my father. We were a little excited because we were very curious to find out what was going on, but we were also a bit nervous. Something truly extraordinary must be happening. As usual, the anchorwoman in her traditional Korean outfit, in the middle of Pyongyang with the Taedong River in the background, appeared on screen. But this evening, she carried a sullen look on her face, like she was on the verge of crying.

"President Kim Il-sung has died," she announced suddenly, fighting back tears.

My father was paralyzed from shock. The anchorwoman might as well have told us that the sky had just collapsed. My sister and I watched our father nervously. The images being displayed on the television had us all stupefied. I didn't really understand everything that was going on, but I knew something unimaginable must have just happened.

Shortly afterward, my mother came home from work in tears. I'd never seen her like this before. At the hospital, she had learned of the news with her coworkers, and one of them had suffered a heart attack from the shock. On that day, many people across the country died from shock. My mom was devastated, because she loved our president with all her heart. In Pyongyang, when she was a child, she had gone to school near Mangyongdae, the little farmhouse where Kim Il-sung was born. Going to Kim Il-sung's birthplace has become a national pilgrimage for North Koreans; I visited it myself when I was very little. My mom told me that once, Kim Il-sung himself visited them at school— my mom stood within one meter of him! He was very tall and had a warm smile, according to my mother. He always looked very cheerful and friendly on the pervasive portraits of him throughout the country, like the one sitting above the entrance to the train station at Eundeok.

He was a god to us, and the mere possibility that he could die seemed unthinkable. Could we still live without our god? Without our father? He was the man who had liberated us from the clutches of Japanese rule, he was the founder of our nation, he was the father of all North Koreans. When his death was announced, daily life took a hiatus across the entire country until the funeral, which was televised a few days later. All around North Korea, scenes of mass hysteria broke out: soldiers rolled around on the floor in tears, women yelled in anguish. On the TV screen, the rain falling behind her, the anchorwoman explained that "even the sky was mourning the death of the Great Leader."

❖

Today, even as I am living in the heart of Seoul, this phrase continues to resonate in my mind, because for me, it represents the indoctrination that we were subjected to and that is still in full force in North Korea. That day, on July 8, 1994, I truly did believe that the sky was crying from despair at the death of Kim Il-sung. I know now, of course, that the downpours were because we were in the middle of monsoon season, and it always rains a lot in Korea during that time of year. But at the time, I was completely brainwashed and believed everything I heard in school and at home. There was no reason for me not to believe—there was no way for me to hear any other version of the truth. Even the adults had no outside information with which to compare what we were learning in school and on TV.

My expatriation has allowed me to unlearn some of the

propaganda fed to us and let me judge reality through my own eyes: my country is ruled under the hands of a blood-thirsty family dynasty. The Kims are not our loving fathers, but are ruthless tyrants. However, today, the overwhelming majority of my fellow countrymen to the north have no way of seeing the truth. My people are completely isolated in a closed-off world. They cannot be blamed if they don't revolt, because they don't know how to form their own opinions and they don't fully understand the true scope of their misfortune. It's difficult to measure the harsh reality of the dictatorship. Internet access is limited exclusively to the highest-ranking members of the Party. Watching foreign television programs, making phone calls abroad, or exchanging mail with foreigners are all strictly forbidden and punishable by imprisonment in one of the country's infamous labor camps.

Nevertheless, largely as a result of bribery, more and more information has been filtering in through the Chinese border, thanks to street vendors and smugglers. But their influence barely makes it past the surface. Along the border between North Korea and South Korea, the world's most heavily militarized border, watchtowers and mines form an impenetrable wall: no messages can reach North Korea except for a few pamphlets denouncing the Kim regime's crimes, sent over the heavily fortified border by balloon. Many families torn apart by the end of the Korean War in

1953 remain without news about their parents who live on the other side of the Demilitarized Zone, or "DMZ." Such is the name given to the barbed barrier that still separates the two sides of the Korean peninsula.

❖

Like everyone else, on the day after Kim Il-sung's death, I was devastated. In the early morning, my mother sent Keumsun and me to the mountains to collect flowers in Kim Il-sung's honor. It was a task that we carried out, just like all the other children in North Korea, on the birthdays of each one of our leaders. If you came back empty-handed, or worse, with yellow flowers, you could get into a lot of trouble. You would become a laughingstock and be punished by the teachers. Yellow was considered the color of our enemies, the Americans. We thought that all Americans were blond, and so we were taught to hate the color yellow.

On this evening, July 9, 1994, there was not a single flower left standing after the children had raided all the flower fields.

As for me, after collecting flowers, I came back and attended a ceremony downtown for public grieving and, in the midst of that frenzy, I started to cry as well. I didn't know exactly why I was crying, but I felt that it was necessary to do so. I remember that standing right next to me, there was a girl who did not manage to actually cry.

She's just pretending, I thought while watching the single tear forming in the corner of her eye. She had no choice but to at least try. She risked being looked down upon if her eyes remained dry.

However, our pain was genuine. We loved Kim Il-sung and his son and successor, Kim Jong-il, with all our hearts. They were to us what Santa Claus is to other children across the world. April 15 and February 16, their respective birthdays, were marvelous days for the kids. We received one kilogram of sweets each on them. The night beforehand, we were always about as excited as we could possibly be, and I could never manage to fall asleep. The morning of their birthdays, with my uniform completely clean, I would proudly go collect my clear plastic bag of goodies with the inscription "We have nothing to envy in the world" written on the exterior. I suppose that this was one way the regime ensured we understood that there was no one happier than us. Inside the bags, there were packs of chewing gum, toffees, sugar-covered soybean paste, and cookies. On the way back, I would hold my bag tight against my body, hidden underneath a cloth that my mom had given me, in order to avoid having my sweets stolen by other children.

❖

Even after I arrived in South Korea, it took me a long time to see the truth about my home country. I did not want to believe that Kim Jong-il was a ruthless dictator. In Seoul, I read a book written by Kim Jong-il's former Japanese cook, who fled to Tokyo to escape from his clutches after having prepared sushi for him for many years. In his book, Kenji Fujimoto recounts in great detail the cruelty of our leader. It was so far from the image of a saintly guardian that I had learned about in school that, at first, I refused to acknowledge what I was reading.

In school, as a child, every morning we would read an anecdote about the exemplary life of Kim Jong-il. In a fairytale-like story, we were told that, on the day he was born, a star appeared above Mount Paektu, the enormous volcano where our nation was founded several millennia ago. We sang songs in praise of our liberator, the great Kim Il-sung. When I visited Pyongyang as a little girl, my dad showed me a tree in a park situated along the Taedong River, which, as a young boy, Kim Il-sung had climbed in order to try to catch a rainbow. I was told that was how he had gotten the idea to launch a socialist revolution.

❖

Today, these lies have been dispelled in my mind. In Seoul, I have learned about the horrific labor camps in my home country, where at least a hundred and fifty thousand prisoners are slowly dying right this moment. I was unaware of the existence of these camps when I lived in North Korea;

I only knew that people were disappearing. In Seoul, you often hear about other defectors who have escaped like I have. I understand now that our country was in fact a vast prison, where the detainees were unaware of the extent of their misfortune, since their first priority was always fighting for their lives.

All of these questions came back to me in November 2010, many years after my escape, when North Korea suddenly bombarded a South Korean island in the Yellow Sea. Four people were killed as a result of the attack, just sixty-six kilometers away from Seoul. My sister and I thought that war was about to break out.

"They are insane!" Keumsun said to me.

For me, I do not believe that there will be an all-out war, just like I don't think the regime will ever give up its power, nor will it abandon its atomic weapons, which it is building in secret. And I constantly wonder if I will ever get the chance to return to North Korea, a North Korea liberated from tyranny and free of pain and hunger.

✤ 5

December 1997

Although my body was as thin as a twig, I still felt like I weighed a ton; my body felt too heavy to move. I slumped onto the hard, frozen ground as the darkness of the night started to swallow me. I no longer had the strength to continue on. My mom had left me. My body remained completely still as I heard footsteps echoing from the staircase. On that cold December night in 1997, when I was eleven years old, I knew that I was going to die before even reaching adolescence.

Suddenly, a muffled sound reached my ears. Was I dreaming? Or was I having a nightmare? I half opened one of my eyes. A dark silhouette appeared before me, its shadow growing larger and larger. Frightened, I lifted myself up, only to see that this shadowy figure looked familiar. Suddenly, I realized it was my mother, along with Keumsun right behind her! I felt a rush of adrenaline jolt through my body and my anguish started to dissipate. I didn't know it was possible to be as happy as I felt in that instant.

Just a few hours ago, I had written my will and testament, and now, here was my family. It was a miracle. I felt a little ashamed for having written the will, especially because my mother and Keumsun were probably already on their way back as I was writing it. I felt like a coward. Worse, I knew I had written some very harsh things to my mom. She found the note, which I had left on the coffee table. I held my breath as she silently read from the page. Her face revealed no emotion, and I will never know what she was thinking in that particular moment. As she read, I could feel my joy slowly fading away.

And then it vanished completely when I realized, much to my dismay, that they had come back empty-handed. Their trip to Rajin-Sonbong had been unsuccessful. They weren't able to bring back any food, and I was starving. I hadn't put anything edible in my mouth since the taste-less concoction of water and dried turnip leaves ran out two days ago. I was terribly disappointed, but did not dare show it.

Mom looked exhausted and distraught after her long, unproductive journey, and reading the note I had left on the table certainly didn't help. There was no food in the apartment, so she just drank a glass of water as her eyes swept around the dark and empty room.

"The only thing left for us to do here is die," she said in a soft, defeated voice. We were all going to die.

Silently, she laid herself down on the patched-up sleeping bag along the wall of the kitchen; it was the least cold place in the apartment. My sister and I huddled next to her. Darkness surrounded us as I started to fall asleep. We were famished and helpless, but at least I wasn't going to die alone.

In the morning, we were awoken by noise from the street, but we didn't move a muscle. Mom was as still as a statue. The burden resting on her shoulders was too much for her to bear. She knew that she was our last hope against the malady that had struck our country and was growing worse each day: the famine. Since 1995, my family members had been slowly dying one after the other, and the three of us were next on the list. Within a span of two years, my mother had lost my grandmother and then my grandfather shortly afterward. Just one month ago, it had been my father's turn to go. Behind her closed eyes, my mom must have been watching this seemingly endless nightmare replay over and over again in her mind.

❖

I had not eaten the cold noodles that I liked so much in over a year. Right up until 1994, I had always had enough to eat because, as I mentioned before, my mother would bring leftovers home from the cafeteria at the hospital. Thanks to her, we ate rice with *kimchi*, a spicy fermented cabbage, on a regular basis. *Kimchi*, a Korean specialty, stings your tongue a little when you eat it but packs a lot of flavor. Once you're accustmed to it, you cannot have a meal without it. But, starting when I was nine years old, we no longer had rice every day. At the hospital, foodstuffs were becoming scarcer. Instead of rice, Mom made us a mushy porridge of corn that I never liked very much.

"I don't want it," I would grumble whenever she put a bowl of the mushy porridge in front of me.

But ultimately, I knew that if I didn't eat that porridge, there was nothing else I could use to fill my stomach.

About the same time that the hospital started running out of food, the state-owned store near our apartment became utterly useless. It was a tiny cement shop with steel bars over its two windows, and it looked more like a prison than a store. All provisions in the town had to pass through this store, because in North Korea, everything belonged to the state, according to traditional socialist dogma. From school uniforms to oil and rice, you were, in principle, supposed to be able to find everything you needed there. But most of the time, it was completely empty. For about two years, the store was nearly always closed due to a lack of supplies. Little by little, the rations distributed to the factory became more and more irregular, until they stopped entirely. As a result, everyone learned to get by in the black market, buying or selling whatever they could at the *jang-madang*, the market tacitly tolerated by the authorities. People sometimes even sold goods on the streets. Everyone put on display in front of their houses what few possessions they had left, which they would sell in order to buy food, whose prices were soaring.

❖

Since escaping North Korea, I have learned that we were victims of the "Great Famine" that devastated my country in the middle of the 1990s. To this day, no one knows exactly how many people perished in this tragedy, which the government denies ever happened. At least five hundred thousand lost their lives. Perhaps the real figure is more than a million, according to some NGOs. In Seoul, I've learned that my province, North Hamgyong, was the most affected by the national disaster.

The causes of this famine are complex. First, the fall of the Soviet Union in 1991 destabilized the North Korean economy; factories, lacking electricity, stopped functioning, fertilizer disappeared from the fields, and food rations became reduced. In 1994, huge floods were the final coup de grâce to the moribund agriculture of my province. The little produce that remained was reserved for military personnel and those of the elite class, while the rest of the population suffered in silence. Young children were the first to succumb to the famine, followed by the elderly and, finally, women. The quality of rations had not stopped deteriorating since I was born during the mid-1980s but, starting from 1994, the quantities also declined drastically, and deliveries were regularly canceled. Officially, the managers of our neighborhood store told us there were just delays. However, sometimes we didn't receive anything for up to six months at a time.

In 1995, in Chongjin, my grandmother was the first to lose the battle against the famine. The next year, my grandfather, a retired military man, also died as a result of the food deprivation. His poor health could not withstand the end of the government rations. My mother learned about what happened via a letter that arrived months after their funerals had already taken place. Due to the inefficiency of the postal service, my mom was never able to say goodbye to her father.

With her eyes closed, lying on the kitchen floor that terrible night in December 1997, she must have been playing all of this back and forth in her head.

Ironically, my family paid dearly as a result of our "privileged" status and our blind loyalty to the state system. We would never have imagined that the regime would allow us to die of hunger. We depended entirely upon government rations to feed us, and thus succumbed more quickly than others who had learned to develop alternative methods of survival. Only those who had developed black-market sources of money had the means to buy food, and only the highest-ranking officials and military personnel had access to government provisions. Alas, it was the middle-ranked officials, like my grandfather, who suffered the most when the rations ended. He also had had no business sense, and had shown himself incapable of undertaking alternate methods of ensuring his survival.

And then, during the summer of 1997, my father couldn't take the hunger anymore. His feeble body had already weakened visibly since the factories stopped handing out food rations. I still remember his face sinking more and more into his skull. One night when he was bringing home a load of coal for us to reheat, he collapsed from fatigue right before my mother's eyes.

"People do strange things right before they die," or so goes an old North Korean adage. In his last days, my father began to fall apart. He would do things that drove my mother crazy. Once, when she came back from work, my mom found the apartment completely empty. She was frantic; she thought we had been robbed. In fact, what had happened was that our neighbors had convinced my dad to give them our possessions to sell in the market. Furious, my mother went straight to the *jangmadang* to retrieve our most valuable items, like the beautiful quilts she had received as wedding gifts. Unfortunately, it was too late; they had already been sold.

One day later, my dad collapsed once again, and this time, he never recovered. We didn't even have enough money to pay for a proper burial. His tomb was just a hole dug in the mud, and all we could do was leave a plank of wood with his name written on it, so that his death wouldn't go unremarked, so that he wouldn't be forgotten, at least not too quickly. A few weeks later, someone stole the wooden plank. Most likely they wanted to use it as firewood— people were ready to do just about anything to ensure their survival.

After my father passed away, our life became a veritable hell, with survival as our sole aim. Even the hospital had nothing left to feed its patients, and no one was receiving any provisions from the government anymore. As I said earlier, Keumsun and I had stopped going to school, because we were no longer presentable. Moreover, we didn't have much time to devote to studying; our days were dedicated entirely to finding something to eat.

The three of us—my mom, Keumsun, and I—lived se-
cluded in the apartment, hidden from public view. Every
night, we snuck out to the fields to steal rice and corn. We
would sneak out armfuls of crops and then go farther up
the mountains, away from the eyes of military or government officials, to separate the grains. We also looked for
roots and mushrooms. Sometimes, we went to chop wood,
which was getting harder and harder to find, to sell as firewood in order to buy sustenance.

Mom took care of chopping down the trees with an
ax, while Keumsun and I kept ourselves occupied with thin-
ner branches to make little bundles of sticks. It was extremely hard work, especially given the weak state of our
bodies. Fortunately, we were never caught in the act.

❖

That terrible night in December 1997, Mom, with her eyes
closed, lay motionless on the makeshift sleeping bag. All
of these memories were undoubtedly playing back and forth
in her head.

The trip to Rajin-Sonbong had been our last hope. As
she was leaving through the doors of our apartment, my
mom had thought that she would be able to bring us back
food, or at least a way to make money and save us all. But
this last attempt had failed.

By morning, my mom still hadn't budged, but, strangely, I felt like she was silently devising a plan in her head. Outside, the sun was already shining brightly. Suddenly, she stood up, a determined look in her eyes. She had decided to take action. Her will to survive had just kicked in.

6

That morning, Mom crossed the point of no return. I saw her stand up, with a look of burning determination in her eyes that contrasted sharply with the despair she had displayed the day before. She was about to do what I would never have imagined possible. She walked straight toward the wall where the portraits of our leaders were hanging, stood up on the tips of her toes, reached out her arms, and removed the portraits of Kim Il-sung and Kim Jong-il; those colored photos of our leaders protected by glass and encased in brown wooden frames. Our two leaders had watched us night and day since my early childhood, like they did in every household in North Korea. Their portraits were everywhere in the country, in every building and on every train in the subway system of Pyongyang. In the quasi-religion invented by Kim Il-sung, these portraits were considered holy objects.

My mom no longer cared. She carefully removed the two sacred portraits of our leaders from their cases, and then took the frames apart. The wooden frames were our last sellable items. In taking them apart, my mom had just committed a crime punishable by death. We had to make sure no one figured out where these sticks of wood had come from. If our neighbors found these pictures outside of their frames, they could denounce us to the regime for "insulting" the two leaders. To be safe, my mom burned the photos.

Mom sold the wooden posts from the frames at the market, and with the money she received in exchange, we were finally able to buy ourselves a meal. For the first time in three days, I had something edible to put in my mouth. My mom seemed to have gotten a little bit of energy back. She decided she would also sell our dresser, our last piece of furniture other than the coffee table on which I wrote my will. But at the *jangmadang*, the black market, the merchants said that the dresser was in too poor condition to sell. The only solution was to chop it up with the ax and turn it into firewood.

But beyond that meager plan, everything was still unknown. How would we survive? The rough winter gave my mother no chance to rest. She also became ill at this time.

She could no longer provide for us, so she sent me away to stay with a friend. I left the house not knowing whether I would ever come back. Keumsun took the train and went to Chongjin to stay with an aunt. Mom needed some time to recover her strength. The neighbors worried about her deteriorating health, especially since it was less than five degrees Fahrenheit outside. They said that the ghost of my father would come back to try to take my mother with him. You always had to be wary of ghosts in North Korea. There were plenty of them, and I was always very afraid of them when I was little.

❖

It was during these last few weeks of winter 1997–1998 that my life took a sharp turn. As we became more and more desperate for food, my mom started to think about the unthinkable: fleeing the country. She began planning to escape from North Korea and head toward unknown territory to save her two daughters. I returned home to see her again at the beginning of February when she started to feel better, and when I saw her, I knew immediately that she had already made the frightening decision: we were going to head to China.

❖

Eundeok is located just one hour away from the Chinese–North Korean border, but we had never imagined taking such a risk. Illegally crossing this border, which was patrolled by guards armed with guns and instructed to shoot on sight, seemed insane. Some of our friends had been quietly advising us to take this risk and cross into China. They told us that there was no chance of survival for us here. They told us stories of several families who had escaped into China and were doing just fine. At first my mom didn't believe them because, when she was young, our country was in fact better off than China. In her younger days, it was the Chinese who dreamed of coming to North Korea to alleviate their hunger. How quickly things change! Furthermore, we in North Korea did not have any information about the rest of the world, other than what was fed to us through the state's propaganda, which always emphasized that it was far better to live here than in the chaos of the capitalist world. We grew up in one big lie, but I didn't know it then.

At long last, though, my mom was convinced. After all, we didn't have much left to lose. And once my mother has an idea in her head, it's impossible to change her mind. Without uttering another word, she started making the proper preparations. We were going to become defectors, traitors to our country. However, at this point, our concerns were far from political. We were guided by our instinct for survival, not by the idea of revolting against the regime. Our only goal was to find food and survive. I had no desire to criticize the dictatorship of Kim Jong-il; I just wanted to alleviate my hunger. It was only later, at the end of our long, perilous journey in search of freedom, that my eyes were opened to the subservience of our lives in North Korea and that I began to understand the horror of that inhumane regime. Today, I can openly denounce the regime's crimes, because I am safely in South Korea. And here, at long last, my stomach is full.

❖

Eighteen years have passed, but I still vividly remember the day that our lives as fugitives began. Our journey would last nine years, but I could not have known it then.

Night was falling over Eundeok. Spring was well on its way but I was still shivering from the cold, because the temperature had dropped when darkness fell. Keumsun, Mom, and I slipped outside. My mother closed the door of our little apartment, this time forever. I brought with me a small backpack with my most precious memories in it: a few photos, particularly the one of my father in which he was wearing an *ushanka*, a fur hat with earflaps, taken in front of the Kim Il-sung statue in Pyongyang. It was one of my favorite pictures of him. On the street around us, the passersby whose paths we crossed were unaware that they would never see us again. Earlier that day, my mom had gone to see a friend to borrow an ax and a saw, under the pretense of needing them to chop some wood. She didn't dare tell her friend that we would be keeping them for good. These two tools would be our key to obtaining food during our journey into the unknown. All we had to do was to chop some wood and sell it whenever we needed food, my mom told us. My mother has always had a strong practical sense.

It was pitch-black out when we reached the village at the Chinese border, after an hour or so of travel on the back of a shaky truck. Cloaked in the darkness of the night, we distanced ourselves from the village and crossed the fields, hiding behind bushes and shrubs. Suddenly, after my eyes became used to the darkness, I saw a sign in the distance that read "Tumen River." Beyond the river was China. Freedom—and what I was hoping for even more, rice—were waiting for us on the other side. Tonight, we would arrive in China.

This spot along the river was familiar because we had made the same trip a few weeks ago. We had made our first attempt to cross the border at the beginning of March. Heeding advice from experienced smugglers, we had intended to cross the frozen river. But we realized when we got there that by then, it was too late. Little chunks of ice were floating along the river. Since the ice was already starting to thaw, we knew we would have to wait until winter of the following year. It seemed like such a long time to wait. After that first attempt, we returned in the dead of night, disheartened, to Eundeok. However, Mom was never one to give up easily, and she decided that we would instead come back in spring to cross the Tumen. And this time, since we had heard that the river wasn't very deep, we would travel through water instead of over ice.

❖

So here we were, on our second attempt. Quietly, we approached the edge of the river. A few meters away from the river, I lay down on the sand. From there, you could observe the border patrols coming and going as they passed through the hills. We stayed still and silent for several hours. Mom was quietly calculating how much time we had between each coming and going of the patrolmen.

Around midnight, after a patrolman had just passed, she gave us the signal and headed toward the sand, and then Keumsun and I followed one after the other. When we reached the river, my feet sank into the freezing water. We had never learned how to swim, but my mom held us tightly. First, the water reached my knees, and then shortly after, it reached right up to my neck. I felt like I was going to be submerged in water. I was so scared. Keumsun and I held on tightly to our still resolute mother. Mom realized that the river was too deep for the two of us, and so we headed back toward the banks of the river on the side we had come from. What a relief!

But my mom is stubborn. She told us to wait for her while

she crossed the river herself and tried to find a path for us. Slowly, her silhouette became fainter and fainter in the distance. My teeth chattered as I watched her fade into the darkness. I was scared she was going to drown and that we'd never see her again. And if she did make it to the other side, what would happen to my sister and me? My heart started pounding as my mother disappeared into the darkness.

Suddenly, after minutes that felt more like hours, Mom reappeared, dripping wet. Her entire body was shivering and she could barely walk. I thought she might faint. She told us that at just two meters away from reaching the Chinese border, she had slipped in the water. I felt helpless. In the darkness of the night, two young girls were by themselves, trying to take care of their sick mother, drenched and chilled from the river.

"So be it. Let's go to the border guards," my mom said in defeat.

7

The chief of police came to meet us in front of the small patrol station near the border. Mom explained that we had left our home to chop wood with the intention of selling it at Rajin-Sonbong, which is why we had to surreptitiously cross the river. I got the feeling that he didn't believe even for a second the lie that we were telling. After a moment of hesitation, he told us to go wait in a corner. We were exhausted and shivering. The officer brought us some pancakes made of cornmeal and some milk powder and let us sleep on the floor. I started warming up again as my body made contact with the *ondol*, the under-ground heating system used in Korea. I fell into a deep, dreamless sleep.

The next morning, I realized how lucky we were. The border official let us leave without any further questions.

At various points throughout our entire journey, we sometimes came across people who were very generous to us, who sympathized with us. I don't even know their names, but without them, I might not be alive today. I want to take the opportunity here to truly thank them from the bottom of my heart.

❧

But in spite of this unexpected generosity from the border guard, our situation was still quite dire. Going back to Eundeok was not an option, my mom decided. We couldn't risk going back when our neighbors knew about our attempted escape. And besides, there would still not be any food for us there. Going back to Eundeok would mean starvation for all of us. But then where were we to go from here? Mom decided that we should head to Rajin-Sonbong, thinking that we would be able to find a means of survival there. We sold the ax and the saw for a bit of pocket money, and then we took off.

I will always remember this day as one of the saddest days of my life. It was raining heavily, we didn't know where we were going to sleep, and we were full of gloom. Worst of all, that photo of my father had been ruined forever. It was my favorite and the last one I had of him. The photo hadn't survived our trip through the Tumen River. The ink had become smudged, and the image of his face, the last memory of his existence, was gone forever. Even to this day, I still miss that photo. In my new life, I have to fight hard to keep the fuzzy memories I have of him from fading away, so that I don't let myself forget about my father. I think again and again about the trip we took to Pyongyang when I was nine. We rode the subway, and then we went to see the statue of Kim Il-sung and his gigantic mausoleum. Dad had wanted to show me all the beautiful things that could be found in the capital city. During that trip, for the first time in my life, he bought me a little toy from a toy store: a small plastic star that I took with me everywhere. I was so proud to show it off in front of my friends at school. These are the memories that I never want to forget.

❖

On that dreary March day after our failed escape attempt, my mother, Keumsun, and I wound up at the Rajin port, where the fishermen unload their cargoes of crab. The most savory and expensive part of the crab was their claws, reserved only for wealthy Chinese merchants. All we could afford were the shells, which were sold at a more modest price. This was the first day of our new, homeless life, and my mom bought several of the shells to help keep our spirits up. The three of us feasted on our crabmeat without thinking about our future or about where we were going to sleep.

Nobody in Rajin could help us, so we left that city to go ask my mom's family in Chongjin for help. It took two days on the train, which was as crowded and as slow as usual, to get to Chongjin, which was over a hundred kilometers to the south. Since we didn't have enough money to buy actual tickets, we snuck onto the back of the train. As the train rattled back and forth, I crouched in a corner to avoid the conductors. Each time they walked by, we pushed through the tightly packed crowd and hid in the restroom. It was no easy feat. We were packed like sardines. The smell of urine was unbearable because a lot of people relieved themselves before they were able to reach the toilets. Plus, you always had to be careful about thieves, of which there were plenty, especially when passing through the dark tunnels. We held our shoes while we slept to be sure that no one would steal them.

It was such a contrast to the luxurious train we had taken to Pyongyang with my dad when I was younger. That train had had upholstered seats, large windows through which you could admire the countryside, and a pleasant atmosphere. Young, attractive women worked as the conductors. During the ride, they would come entertain us by playing the accordion in the central aisle. Passengers would often make song requests, which the conductors would gladly fulfill, but not before asking the voyager who had made the request to sing along. There was even a built-in restaurant on the train.

For the rest of my life, I will treasure that memory, even though I know now that the luxury was just a mirage meant to maintain the image of our country's dictators. The food shortages were already in full force throughout the rest of the country at that time. But I could ignore them, during that trip. I felt happy just to revel in the carefreeness of childhood.

After the exhausting two-day journey, we knocked on the door of my aunt, my mother's younger sister. She was speechless at seeing us dressed like homeless people. My aunt had not heard from us in a long time, but she would never have imagined seeing us like this.

Very quickly, we understood that we were not welcome. My aunt wanted to help us, but her husband had other ideas in mind. Unfortunately, in North Korea, it is the man of the household who calls the shots. Two hours later, we were asked to leave. The famine had resulted in a vicious game of every man for himself.

My mother was shocked. She had helped my aunt so many times in the past. When my mom had worked at the hospital, she frequently sent her sister rice cakes and other provisions through the postal service that was, at the time, more functional. And yet there we were, shoved outside without even so much as a parting gift.

Distraught, Mom went by herself to gather her thoughts at her father's grave. After this failure, she did not dare go bother her youngest sister, her favorite, who also lived in Chongjin. Disappointed, we went back to the station and took the crowded train heading back north toward the desolation of Rajin-Sonbong. One by one, every door was closing behind us. Our plan to escape to China over the frozen Tumen had to be pushed back at least until the next winter. And so, shamefully, we began our homeless life. We had not left our miserable little residence in Eundeok just to return to it again.

❖

I remember very clearly an especially shameful incident that occurred as I was walking on a street in Rajin during the time we lived there. Suddenly, a small boy appeared behind me.

"*Kojebi!* You're a *kojebi!*" he said, sneering, looking me straight in the eyes. I was overwhelmed by anger. I left my belongings on the sidewalk and, furiously, I chased after him.

"I am not a *kojebi!*" After a mad dash, the boy disappeared in the labyrinth of the streets. I came back to my sister, having been unsuccessful in my pursuit. I was visibly shaken up. I started to feel an immense sadness. *Kojebi* is a word of Russian origin. In North Korea, it denotes a homeless child. In Eundeok, I had seen more and more of them appear, and my parents would always tell me to be wary of them. These orphans were the result of the great famine. Since the beginning of the 1990s, many children had lost their parents to hunger. They had to learn how to survive alone on the streets, suffering from the complete indifference of a regime that let its people fall victim to misery and famine, all while giving the international aid it received to the army and the privileged class. Even to this day, these *kojebi* children organize into gangs and steal whatever they can. This is the side of North Korea that the regime keeps hidden, that the propaganda is careful not to show.

I had never felt so insulted in my life as when that boy jeered at me in the street. But worst of all, even worse than being called a *kojebi*, was the realization that it was indeed true. I had truly become a *kojebi*, a child of the streets.

❖

After our failed escape attempt in the spring, the three of us lived a homeless life in Rajin for many months, often going several weeks at a time without being able to bathe. Lice infested our heads and we scratched at them like monkeys. Every night, we had to find new shelter where we could sleep and escape from the foggy rain that clouded the summer. When night fell and all the merchants left, we would slip under an awning that we found at the front of the market. But often an official would come to tell us to leave. So then we would take shelter in the staircases of nearby buildings. The smell from the restrooms around us reeked, but at least we had shelter. That is, until the building managers asked us to leave. After we had been kicked out of everywhere else, our last option was to sleep under a bridge.

When the rain stopped, my mother took us to the forest to sleep under the stars. It was better this way, far from the scathing eyes of others. More important, we could bathe ourselves in the streams and rid ourselves of the thick grime that had collected on us. This also let us save some time, since we were right next to our workplace. Collecting wood had effectively become our means of sustenance. Every morning we participated in this task, which I always hated. We didn't have any tools, so using all of our strength, we pulled branches off trees using our bare hands. It was exhausting, and all for a mediocre result, since at the market stands, our handmade sticks paled in comparison to the ones cut with a saw. We rarely got more than ten or fifteen won. To earn more, Mom came up with a clever trick. She put me, the youngest of the family, behind the display. With my small frame and miserable appearance, I got the pity of buyers who would feel bad haggling with such a poor, helpless girl.

❖

Every day, we had to go to the market and at night return to the countryside, often with empty stomachs. One day,

I couldn't take it anymore. The heavy stick I was carrying was tearing into my shoulder. I had no energy left and I refused to move another inch.

"We have to get to the market and sell these before nightfall!" exclaimed my mother.

I didn't move.

"Fine, stay there. We're going to continue," said my mother in exasperation.

I watched as they became smaller and smaller in the distance, and I let myself fall to the ground. It was decided: I was going to spend the night right here on the ground, alone. I was barely twelve years old.

The darkness came quickly and enveloped me entirely, making me regret my decision almost immediately. The noise that the leaves made as the wind rustled through them frightened me. I kept thinking I had heard someone coming closer, or that I saw shadows moving behind the trees. To drown out everything else, I plugged my ears and closed my eyes.

It was impossible to sleep. I reopened my eyes and looked toward the sky. Pale moonlight piercing through the clouds lit up the night. To take my mind off the spookiness of the forest, I focused my attention on the giant fluffy masses in the sky. Little by little, I started to make out some strange images in them. There was a dragon, a man . . . I was filled with amazement and slowly started to forget about my fear.

Since that night, I've never seen another night sky as beautiful as that one. Then I started to become as sleepy as a newborn baby. In the morning, I awoke, still alone in the forest, but otherwise feeling fine. Then I heard footsteps in the distance. From the bushes, my mother and Keumsun emerged. I was filled with joy to see them. Best of all, they hadn't come back empty-handed. They brought *tteok*s, rice cakes. My secret wish was about to be realized: we were going to enjoy some delicious food and have a marvelous day.

❖

In Rajin, the weather dictated our daily lives and my mother adapted our strategies for survival accordingly. The day after a sea storm, we would head to the beach to collect seaweed that had washed ashore. Using the seaweed we collected, we made a soup to sell at the market. At the harbor, I fetched the fish that the fishermen threw away. One afternoon, near a storage facility, the smell of apples filled my nose. Searching through the facility, I found an entire crate full of apples, many of them rotten, abandoned by Chinese merchants. I took out the ones that were still fresh, and on that afternoon, we feasted.

This lifestyle was exhausting, however. The summer was coming to an end; the foggy mist of the summer was being replaced by a vast blue sky populated by immense clouds.

In North Korea, we say that the sky becomes bigger in September. I celebrated my twelfth birthday on the streets, and we were still without hope for the future.

One day, I met another *kojebi* boy. As we were talking on the sidewalk, he shared some tips on how to make it on the streets:

"We steal. Stealing provides us with the means to make money, especially when we steal cabbage. Sometimes we get up to five hundred won for each robbery!"

I understood right away it would be in my family's best interests to change our tactics. Our incessant trips back and forth to the mountains, our feeble attempts to snatch a few branches off the trees, our business of selling wood utterly exhausted us, and all for nothing, or at least not for much. Forget morale. If we wanted to make it out of North Korea, we needed money.

So we started stealing as well. We stole whatever we could: vegetables, cabbage, and corn that we resold at the market. This helped us make a bit of money on the side. But it was a risky business. One morning, while we were snatching a few potatoes, some farmers appeared. We were caught red-handed. My mother begged for them to spare us. They didn't listen to a word she said and started violently beating her right in front of us. Keumsun and I were horrified as we awaited our turn. Luckily, they didn't touch us. We looked too frail and defenseless. Fortunately, they also didn't send us to the police. That was a close call, and we only narrowly escaped.

After this misadventure, my mother racked her brains to find a less risky way to survive. She dreamed of starting a small business with her youngest sister. So, in the fall, she sent me once more to Chongjin, this time with five hundred won in my pocket—quite a large sum at the time. It was enough to buy ten kilograms of corn. I was to convince my aunt to come join us. Even if she said no, Mom told me to stay in Chongjin, because she couldn't afford to take care of me anymore in Rajin.

❖

I took the train by myself. I was no longer afraid, because I had been hardened by my experience as a *kojebi*. My aunt welcomed me with open arms and, thanks to the five hundred won I brought with me, she was able to provide me with good food. Then, carefully, I started to tell her about our plan. Though initially frightened by the idea, my mother's favorite sister started to think it over. She and her husband were having problems in their marriage and argued all the time.

Two days later, the two of us stood at the train station waiting to catch the train to Rajin-Sonbong. We were relatively at ease, because we didn't think anyone knew about my aunt's intent to run away. Suddenly, through the crowd of passengers in the station, we noticed her husband, frantically running around in search of her. We quickly hid ourselves, our hearts racing. My aunt was clearly anguished. She hesitated. Then the train arrived. Right as we were about to get on, my aunt took a step back.

"You know, I do have a husband and two children, after all. I can't just leave them here."

I didn't have any way of convincing her out of it; she had made her decision. All I could do was say to her, "If you ever change your mind, come meet my mom in Rajin. Wait in front of the train station. We always pass by there."

The train shook back and forth, and I left by myself. Even today, this memory still haunts me. I have not heard from my aunt, or from the rest of my family, since then. Is she still in Chongjin, alive? Or has she died from hunger? Feelings of guilt follow me everywhere. By saying that she was always welcome to stay with us in Rajin, I made her an implicit promise: that she could depend on us. What if she came to the train station and waited for us, only to find that no one was there? I will never know, because a month later, we left Rajin for good.

When I arrived back in Rajin, my mom realized that there wasn't a future for us anymore in our country. The first winter frost was starting to trickle in. Soon, it would be too cold to survive on the streets. But the cold provided us with another opportunity: the Tumen River would freeze over and become solid enough for us to cross.

❖ 8

During that frigid night, a pale glow hung over the trees. At the top of the hill, a wisp of gray smoke rose up in the air until it faded into the darkness. We walked closer to the source of the smoke, since we needed to stay warm. We climbed through the forest toward this mysterious glowing fire. It was bitterly cold out, and the strong February winds slapped me in the face. Around the small fire, we were slowly able to make out two crouched figures: a man and a young girl. After seeing how desperate they looked, I thought that maybe they were trying to do the same thing we were—escape the country. My mother started talking to the man, and he confirmed what I suspected. That night, with his daughter, who was even younger that I was, he was planning to risk it all to leave North Korea.

"The ice is hard enough. I've seen people crossing it," he told us.

Finally, some good news.

"But it's better to wait until the early morning," he advised us. "The guards don't patrol as much then."

We were almost at the top of a hill that looked out over the Tumen River. It was the perfect spot to observe the border guards as they walked back and forth. Right in front of us, through the darkness, was China. Our last chance. Our last obstacle was to cross this frozen river, patrolled by guards armed with guns and with instructions to shoot on sight. Hours passed by. My anxiety started to build. I remembered our previous failure. What if this time the soldiers shot us down?

❖

Five hours later, the riverbanks were eerily calm. There was no one in sight. It was our sign to take off. Silently, the five of us headed down the hill, through the forest, toward the Tumen. There were still no guards in sight. The man tested the ice using his foot, to make sure that it really was frozen. The ice appeared solid, covered with a thin blanket of snow. As a precaution, we walked single file, several meters away from one another, to spread our weight evenly along the ice. My mom was the first, followed by Keumsun, then the man and his young daughter. Finally, I started trekking as well. I was the last and did not dare turn back. Behind my back, the ink-black night looked like it was going to snatch me away. I imagined a border guard appearing at any moment and shooting at us. We only had about a hundred meters to cross, but it felt like an eternity. What would happen if I was the only one who didn't make it to the Chinese side? My heart pounding, I started moving faster. Suddenly, I lost my balance. I fell several times while crossing over this slab of ice. As a result, we started walking more slowly, at a turtle's pace, much slower than we had planned. The light of dawn was already starting to surface. We had to hurry. Just a few more meters to go. I caught up to everyone else, and thought that we were safe.

In reality, we were merely on a small islet on the river. We still had to cross several meters on the other side of the river, where the ice looked less solid.

From there, we rearranged our order. The little girl, the lightest, was to start, with me behind her. Timidly, she approached the other side. Suddenly, we heard a huge cracking sound. The young girl had just sunk through the ice right before our eyes. We started panicking and began to head back to the islet. Her legs were submerged up to her knees. She started screaming.

"Have you reached the bottom?" asked her father.

"Yes," she responded in a frightened voice.

So despite the cold, we started wading through the icy

water that burned our skin. We moved forward...just a few more meters, and my feet touched China.

We had finally made it.

I stopped to catch my breath, but my wet clothes had already started to freeze.

We took a few moments of rest, but soon fear overtook us again. We had to get as far away from the river as we could, because if the Chinese police found us, they would send us right back to North Korea. I didn't even want to think about the terrible punishments we would receive back in North Korea if we were caught. We didn't have a minute to lose. Before us, there were fields of corn stretching as far as the eye could see. We had to pass through these fields as quickly as we could to reach the hills in the forest. But my leg was stiff from the cold and I couldn't run. Using all the strength I had left in me, I tried to follow my mom's pace. The hills felt so far away. Finally, after about ten minutes, we made it. I collapsed beneath the trees as the sky began to get light. The sun was shining. It was my first morning outside of my home country.

The first dawn of my new life.

❖

How would the Chinese treat us? I didn't know anything about this country. Hidden behind the trees, I observed the landscape. On the road below, I noticed some men and women on bicycles. They were most likely off to work. This was the first time I'd ever seen Chinese people. On the other side of the road, there were little houses with gardens. This seemed to confirm what our neighbors had told us: China was a rich country. In North Korea, it was rare to own a house, because people usually lived in apartment buildings. I found this new world both strange and fascinating. As a child, I never would have believed that one day I would leave my country behind.

All of a sudden, a man on a bicycle appeared in front of us. He motioned for us to come closer and said something in a language that I couldn't understand. We started panicking. Would he denounce us to the authorities? Immediately, we took off and headed toward the forest without knowing where we were going. Our only objective was to get as far away as possible from the border. After running for quite some time, we were surrounded by silence. We were in the middle of nowhere. I was terribly cold in my frozen-solid clothes. So we stopped right there. The man who had escaped across the river with us made a small fire. I collapsed from exhaustion near the campfire. The heat from the flame felt heavenly. After such a tumultuous night, it was a blessing to finally be able to sleep.

That afternoon, we woke and began walking again, still without knowing where we were going. Our priority was to find something to eat. We were gripped by hunger. As night fell again, we had still not found anything with which to fill our stomachs. We had come to China in order to find food, and here we were, about to starve all over again.

Desperate, my mom knocked on the door of a house on the edge of a small village. Miraculously, a woman opened the door and offered us something to drink . . . and she spoke in Korean! Apparently, in this region along the border, much of the population was originally Korean. We had arrived at the house of the village's mayor, who welcomed us in with a feast of rice, dumpling soup, and an especially delicious dried tofu. It was left over from the Chinese New Year celebration. The mayor was friendly, but he also gave us a warning.

"Eat everything that you can, and then return to North Korea," he told us. "It's not safe here for people like you. You will be arrested."

We did not listen to him. Returning to North Korea was not an option for us. So we slept that night at a construction site in the village.

❖

At the crack of dawn the next morning, I was awoken by a loud commotion around me. The father of the little girl explained to me that some people from the neighboring village had come to find my mother. They were talking with her quite loudly. I felt uneasy about what was happening.

Abruptly, my mom turned toward me and looked me right in the eyes.

"These people know a couple who want to adopt a child," she murmured.

I could hardly understand what she was saying.

"If you want to go with them, you can..." she said, in a pained voice.

I started feeling lightheaded.

Mom tried to convince me. "You will definitely have a better life with them than with me. I don't have much left to take care of you with."

Hearing these words, I almost fainted. I would follow my mom's suggestion if I had to, but I was so heartbroken to hear those words from her—it felt like she was ready to abandon me.

Luckily, the villagers discovered that I was already twelve years old, despite my young appearance. I was too old for the couple and thus had to stay with Keumsun and Mom.

However, our situation now was just as bad as it had been in Rajin-Sonbong. Later that day, the man who had escaped with us and his young daughter left us to go and stay with his parents. We were alone. We had thought that once we crossed the border, everything would somehow magically sort itself out for us. In reality, we were worse off than we had been back home, because here we were living in hiding and at risk of being arrested by the police at any instant.

In fact, Beijing had signed an agreement with its ally Kim Jong-il, stipulating that China was obligated to send back anyone who tried to escape from North Korea. As a result, tens of thousands of North Koreans still live in hiding in Chinese territory, in fear of being caught by the police at any moment. To this day, Chinese authorities ignore the requests of South Korea and of NGOs to provide asylum for North Korean defectors. When we first arrived in China, we were there without a roof over our heads and without food, in addition to fearing that the locals would denounce us.

❖

How long would we be able to last? I asked myself during my afternoon nap that first day in China, as I lay alongside a rice field. Suddenly I felt a presence there next to me, and I opened my eyes. It was a man, standing right above me. I sprang up, with Keumsun and Mom following me. We saw that there was a woman on a bicycle with the man, as well.

"Don't be afraid, I can help you," she said in Korean.

Instinctively, we fled to hide in an empty farm. But the woman found us again.

"I will help you, I swear! Come with me!"

She sounded kind enough. And at that point we didn't have much to lose, so we followed her. At her house, we celebrated her mother-in-law's eightieth birthday. We were embarrassed about our dirty clothing, so we just stuck to ourselves in a corner. The woman found us some new, clean clothes and then sent us in a taxi that dropped us off in a small village where everything was unfamiliar.

We were shivering the entire journey. But once we arrived at the village, we were put in a small house and provided with food from our guardian angel for three days. I started to recover my strength. It felt so good to be warm again. We stayed in a farmhouse, protected by metal bars. I learned that we were in the middle of Hunchun, one of the important towns of this region that shares a border with North Korea, not very far from the Tumen River. In front of the house, there was no garden, but there was a pigsty where several pigs were grunting and rolling around in the mud. Inside the farmhouse, there were only two rooms. The smaller one was reserved for our savior's two children, whom she took excellent care of. In the bigger room, the five of us—Keumsun, my mom, and I; as well as the woman taking care of us, and her husband—slept on mattresses on the floor.

We felt very lucky—this woman seemed so generous. After meeting her, I felt my spirits lift. I was anxious about our future, so I clung to her in the hope that she could save us. In the span of just a few days, I had realized that life in China was dangerous for refugees like us, living in hiding. Without our hostess, we would be at risk for the worst dangers, particularly arrest. Furthermore, I could not take the chance of crossing the walls next to the pigsty. Behind the walls was the street, where we risked being denounced. So we snuggled comfortably behind these protective walls. But I quickly started to grow bored, since there was nothing to do and no games to play. All I could do to keep myself entertained was to watch the pigs play around in the mud. At least they didn't have the same worries that we did.

Little by little, the woman earned our trust, and she and my mom started developing a friendship. They talked a lot in the bigger room. Secretly, I listened to them as they spoke.

"I know how to ensure your future," said the woman one morning to my mother. "You will be able to live in safety, send your daughters to school . . . and even obtain a *hukou*."

A *hukou*? Was it possible? The *hukou* is a registration document that would grant us permanent residency in China, which would have let us emerge from our lives in hiding.

I listened carefully.

"Marry a Chinese man," our hostess informed my mother. "You know, they look like they wouldn't make great husbands, but they have money and will treat you well."

Mom stayed silent. I was shocked. I listened even more attentively. My mother looked like she was giving this wild proposition some serious thought over the course of their conversation. Our hostess told my mom not to spend too long deciding, and then she gave us a few moments alone to think.

My mom felt a little uneasy as she discussed our options with Keumsun and me. Her thought process was very pragmatic: to survive in this country, she needed to find a job. But how did you find a job without documentation? Getting paid under the table seemed too risky. She also thought it would be better to get married because that would ensure, financially, the education of her two daughters. In China, just like in Korea, society frowned upon a mother living alone and raising her children by herself. If getting married meant obtaining a residency permit, then yes, to find a good husband seemed like the perfect solution to our problems.

At first, I was a bit perplexed by my mom's decision, but I decided that I would respect it and trust her judgment. It was my duty as her daughter, and besides, she knew better than I did what was good for us. Over time, I started to believe as well that marriage was our best chance.

In retrospect, I can say today that this willingness to marry a Chinese stranger might seem difficult to understand, but we were desperate. We wanted to ensure our safety at any cost. In China, we felt like we were being watched at every second. How were we supposed to leave this country without help? The solution proposed by our "savior" seemed to me the only possible option. It was either get married, or get arrested and be repatriated to North Korea, where prison or worse awaited us. Besides, this Chinese woman who'd welcomed us in seemed so nice and so helpful—and she promised us a kind and considerate man. What did we have to lose?

❖

As soon as our guardian angel received my mom's consent, she set to work immediately. She made many calls on her cell phone. Sometimes, she spoke in Korean. When that was the case, I tried to guess what the conversation was about. More often, she spoke in Chinese and I couldn't understand what she was saying. She enthusiastically inquired about every potential suitor. While listening to her talk on the phone, I asked myself, *Is this really how she was going to find us a man?* I thought that she would ask friends, neighbors even. But she seemed instead to have some sort of a network, and a lot of experience as a matchmaker. Were there really that many Chinese men who were looking for North Korean wives?

That morning, she scurried around frantically and just a few hours later, her phone started ringing. Then it rang again. Everything seemed to be moving faster than we had expected. But our "generous savior" never told us any details of the phone calls.

The morning of the third day, two sinister-looking men with dark, sunburned skin appeared in the room where I was staying. One of them had a huge burn on his left temple, and his hair had stopped growing there.

They are both so hideous, I thought in fear, when I saw them standing in front of our hostess in a corner of the kitchen.

I tried to listen to them discreetly, but to no avail. They were speaking in Chinese, and I couldn't understand a word they were saying.

A moment later, the uglier of the two took out a bundle of very dirty money, and gave twenty hundred-yuan bills to our hostess.

The woman came to fetch us and told us to pack our belongings and follow her.

"This man wants a son," she explained to my mother.

I did not yet understand that we had just been sold for two thousand yuan.

* 9

Several Months Later

We never should have come to China. For three hours, my mother, Keumsun, and I had been walking through the darkness of the Chinese countryside looking for a bus stop. To flee . . . to leave this barbaric man who held us prisoner. Mom had decided to flee one night after a particularly nasty argument with her Chinese "husband."

"I want her to give me a son," he had told the woman who sold us to him. For several months, he harassed my mom in this pursuit.

That night, she just couldn't take it anymore.

"I'm too old to get pregnant now, let us go," she begged him.

"I paid two thousand yuan for you, reimburse me then!" he hollered back at her.

❖

From the very first day, I hated this man. He was more than forty years old, but I, a little girl, was already better educated than he was. He didn't even know how to write his own name. He just used an *X* as his signature.

I still remember very clearly the first day of our new life with this man. We had left our "savior" and headed toward unknown territory. Because our "savior" hadn't even bothered telling us which one of the two boorish men had bought us in the kitchen, it took a while to get used to the idea that this would be the new man in our lives, my new "father." Our "savior" barely even said good-bye to us.

We left her house following the two men, who walked in front of us. We didn't exchange even one word. It was only when the three of us were sitting on a bus headed toward an unfamiliar destination, alone with one of the two men, that everything started to sink in. The other man was just a friend of his who had come to help him with the transaction.

My mom's new "husband" wasn't very tall, no doubt less than five foot four, with a protruding stomach mounted atop two tiny legs. He had a square face that was large and flat—there was nothing charming about him whatsoever. I got the feeling that he wasn't very confident in himself, or at least that he was a bit timid. He seemed to want to say something to me, but then changed his mind, as if he was incapable of communicating. But then again, we didn't know how to speak Chinese.

The bus shook back and forth as we rode in silence across the countryside before reaching a small town, where we disembarked. At that station, the man led us to another bus and then we took off again, still having no idea where we were headed. We were on the bus for nearly four hours. Finally, we reached Sukhyun-Jin, another small town in Jilin Province.

When we got there, we were in for quite the surprise: waiting for us there was a small, dirty ox pulling a rickety wagon. To my horror, I realized that we were deep in the Chinese countryside. And to think that the woman had promised my mom a well-established husband in the city.

We traveled at a turtle's pace along a muddy country road in this wretched vehicle, until we reached a scanty village called Yang Chang Chon. With our heads down, we moved down the main street and felt the curious eyes of the villagers glaring at us. I anxiously observed this new scenery, including the houses that were soon to become the scenery of my daily life.

On the other side of the village, the route went up a hill, and right as night was falling, the wagon finally stopped and we disembarked in front of a pitiful-looking farm: our new home. The farmhouse's roof was made of straw and the walls were made of wattle and daub planted atop gravel. It was already dark, and the weather was very gray that day, which only reinforced the negative feelings I already had about this place. Here I was, condemned to live in a slum. And to think that I had heard that China was a land of plenty. Even our apartment in Eundeok had been better than this.

❖

Immediately, from the very first night, we understood that we were not welcome in this family, and that life was not going to be easy—far from the naïve images of comfort and security we'd originally had in mind. We learned that the man still lived with his old parents, whose word, according to Confucian tradition, was law in the household. The man was the third son in a peasant family of six children. His four brothers and his sister had left to go live in the big city, while he was still stuck at the farm. He had once been married, but his wife had fled the farm. He never told us why, but after seeing the way he treated us, I think I could venture a guess.

After arriving at the farm, we saw that my new "father" lived not only with his parents, but also with his nephew and niece. They were wearing dirty, tattered clothes, and the boy limped when he walked—adding all the more to the depressing atmosphere of the household.

The farmer's elderly mother was never fond of having

an outsider as a daughter. Right away, she made it understood that we were merely tolerated in the household and that we had to obey everything she said. The first night, she made us sleep in the stable attached to the tiny house. Before going to bed, we were allowed to eat a greasy Chinese meal with the family. Silently, under the feeble lighting, I forced myself to hide my utter disgust at eating this fatty and indigestible food. Oh how much I missed Korean food, especially *kimchi*. Life here was miserable already.

❖

The next day, our suspicions were confirmed: we were merely three bodies to toil away in the fields every day under the careful watch of the farmer's old mother. On the morning of the first day at the farm, we were already put to work, picking out weeds and planting rice, potatoes, and beans.

For the first few weeks, we tried to just go along with it, and we did the best we could in the fields. We were rather disappointed that we had ended up in such a depressing and backward area, but we didn't have any other options. It was the only way we had been able to improve our living conditions, the only way we could leave the world of begging and avoid getting arrested on the streets. And so we did our best to integrate ourselves into this family and to try to reach a mutual understanding between us and this man. At first, he tried to do the same. He tried to defend us against his irascible mother. We were allowed to move around on the farm, and the four of us could sleep together in one of the three rooms while the man's old parents occupied the room the farthest away. But whenever the man's brothers came back home, we had to return to the stable. Priority went to family, of which we were clearly not a part.

❖

The house was dirty and dilapidated. There was a heating system that was a little like the *ondol* used in Korea but that used firewood instead—it was so archaic you would think it was from another century. We had to heat it up using the fire from the kitchen, the only source of heat in the house. And since the walls were dotted with holes that let in cold air from the outside, it was absolutely frigid during winter, a winter which, in this area in the northeast of China, was just as bad as our winters in North Korea. Snow didn't fall all that frequently, but when it did, the ground stayed white for weeks on end.

The old mother was clearly our enemy, and she started making more and more derogatory comments about us and imposed chores and punishments on us that were often absurd. For her, we were just slaves, and she treated us as if it was already an enormous honor for us to even live under the same roof as her. One day, she drew a line on the ground near the entrance of the house that we, the Koreans, were not allowed to cross. This ridiculous and arbitrary new rule meant that we had to detour around the building to the back whenever we wanted to go out. It was her way of making sure we understood our inferior status.

The man also started imposing more restrictions, quickly forgetting his earlier efforts to help us during the first few weeks. For example, one night, after a long day of hard work in the fields, he refused to let us turn on the TV to watch a show, claiming that it would drive up the electricity bill. Often, after dinner, we would try to assert ourselves and turn on this archaic TV anyway. It was our only time of rest and distraction from a long day of labor. And in response he would get up and turn it off.

"You're going to use up all the electricity if you watch it this much!" he would say without the smallest hint of irony.

After a few months, we started to learn a bit of Chinese, which let us respond to him tit for tat. But that also meant that we started having vicious arguments nearly every day, and that the atmosphere soon became unbearable.

Fortunately, my "stepfather"'s nephew and niece were nice to Keumsun and me. Despite the language barrier, we quickly became friends. First we started playing hide-and-seek on the esplanade in front of the farm. They taught me a Chinese game called *jianzi*, like Hacky Sack, that I really enjoyed. Using our feet, we juggled a small shuttlecock decorated with feathers. I played for hours on this muddy terrain with my friends, whenever I didn't have to work in the fields.

❖

The farm was located on a promontory and we had an excellent view of the road down below. If a police car was coming from Yang Chang Chon, we could spot it from afar and neighbors would have enough time to warn us that it was coming. Indeed, everyone in the village knew where we came from and tried to protect us. As soon as a neighbor gave us warning, sometimes by telephone, we headed out the back of the farm and went to hide in the forest. Often, we would sleep in a cabin for a night or two before returning to the farm after everything settled. We were still, after all, living in China illegally.

Eventually, we had to face reality: our "benefactor," the woman who'd seemed to help us so much when we first arrived in China, had been deceiving us the whole time. This "kind" and "benevolent" woman had not contacted us and had not asked us how we were doing after she pocketed the two thousand Chinese yuan. Not only did she make money behind our backs by selling us like we were commodities, but she didn't keep the promise she had made to us. She had promised my mom an official marriage, which would have allowed us to obtain residency permits in China. If we'd gotten them, my sister and I would have had legal protection here and been able to go to school, which was rather important for us at that age. We had not gone to school since our father died. In reality, this poor farmer had bought us illegally and had no intention of legitimizing the marriage. And he had good reason, because if he let it slip that we were North Koreans, we would immediately be arrested and sent back to our country according to the agreement signed between Beijing and Pyongyang. What's more, this gave him a way of blackmailing us and holding us prisoner. If we tried to leave, we risked being arrested at any moment. But if we'd had residency permits, we would have been able to escape without giving him what he wanted the most: a son.

From the beginning, he never stopped bothering my mom about this. Mom was so embarrassed. She was already in her forties. First she tried to tell him that she could no longer get pregnant. But her new "husband" was insistent; she had no choice but to try anyway, for the sake of her two daughters. She remembered the "agreement" the woman who sold us had mentioned: "This man wants a son."

With no better option available, my mom told us that if she gave him what he wanted, the family would finally accept us and our material well-being would improve. Perhaps we would even have the chance to become legal residents. I didn't know what to think of it all.

The man was always telling my mother what benefits rearing a child would bring. His desire for a son did not stem from affection, but from material reasons. Poor, introverted, stuck on this remote farm, and abandoned by his previous wife, he had devised a plan to help him to reap the benefits of his parents' estate: if he succeeded in having a son, he would be able to snatch the family inheritance, in place of his older brothers. According to Chinese tradition, the inheritance goes to the eldest son of a family. This man was only the third son in his family, but only his younger brother had a son, who was a cripple at that. If my mother gave him the son he wanted, he hoped that his father would give him the family inheritance, especially the farm.

"If we had a son, everything would be different," my mom said to me.

And so, for nearly a year, he tried to get a son out of my mother, but to no avail. The more time that passed the more aggressive and cruel he became with my mom, my sister, and me. And his mother did the same.

"How is it that this Korean woman is incapable of getting pregnant?" his mother would complain whenever my mom walked by. Mom felt hurt and her sense of self-esteem started to diminish. All day, the man would try to humiliate us in public.

For example, I made many friends in the village who

sometimes came over to play. Most of the time, they were boys because there were very few girls in Yang Chang Chon. To control the problem of overpopulation, China had established the "one-child policy," and for the most part, people did not break this rule. But the majority of Chinese families preferred having a boy, which left many mothers seeking abortions if they became pregnant with a girl. This is because when a girl gets married in China, she leaves to live with the family of her husband, and her parents don't have anyone else to take care of them in old age. In Yang Chang Chon, as was the case in many other villages in the Chinese countryside, girls were hard to find.

I had made a lot of friends there. My sister was a bit more reserved and spent most of her time with our mother. I had a lot of fun playing with the neighborhood kids. We played dodgeball using a ball we'd made by filling a bag with corn.

One day, when the Chinese farmer was extremely angry, he hollered at my friends: "Never be friends with this girl! Her mother doesn't know how to behave herself!"

It was truly public humiliation for me. It was infuriating to think that this man, who had bought us, was claiming that my mom behaved poorly. It was all the more unbearable because my friends from the village were my only source of release from the insufferable world of living on the farm. Whenever I think back to my life in China, the times I spent with my friends from the village are, undoubtedly, my best memories.

❖

Then our situation grew even worse. The arguments between my family and the farmer's family, all in Chinese, became more and more frequent. Everyone yelled and screamed every day. My "stepfather" started to become violent. He began regularly hitting my mom, Keumsun, and me. The nightmare seemed to have no end.

During these times, seeing this violent man who was trying to force my mom to bear his son, I couldn't stop myself from thinking about my father, my real father. My father with the frail frame, who was taken away from us by the famine. On the rare occasions when nothing was going on at the farm, I watched the Chinese sky, and I would sometimes see my dad's face in the clouds. He had been so kind, so generous, and so well educated compared to this uncouth Chinese peasant. He had never yelled at us, and it would have been utterly unimaginable for him to hit us.

We couldn't really do anything other than give in to my "stepfather," but there came a day when enough was enough, and we just couldn't take it anymore. Anything would have been better than living in that never-ending nightmare.

It was because of this that my mom finally snapped. After one last dispute with her husband during the night, she decided to take us and leave. It had been nearly a year since we had arrived at the farm.

❖

So there we were, the three of us, walking through the night, without realizing the futility of our mad undertaking. We still faced the issue of not having residency permits. My mom's marriage was, after all, unofficial, and there was no record of it anywhere. We were still in this country illegally. If we come across a police officer, he would arrest us and send us back to North Korea.

My mother realized, a bit too late, that she had given in to a moment of anger and desperation which, although it had been warranted, would put us in danger. We wandered around aimlessly, overcome by doubts and fears of getting arrested. Thoughts were dashing around in my head. What should we do? Oddly, I started to feel a bit of pity for our torturer, the farmer. He was a frustrated man who was violent and sometimes evil, but he was also a victim. He was a broke, miserable man, abandoned by his wife, who dreamed of having a son to gain back his position in the family and in society. This feeling of pity might seem contradictory, especially after all the hardships he had put us through. In Korean, there is a specific term used to define this unalterable link that ties two beings together by both hatred and love. We call it *"cheong."* It's a mysterious connection that bonds two people for the duration of their lives, and that can never be broken no matter what happens.

As we walked, we started to give more and more thought to the idea of turning back. Finally, in the middle of the night, Mom caved in. Just a bit before dawn, we turned around and started heading back to the farm.

In front of the door, the farmer was waiting for us, with a smug look of satisfaction. He must have realized that we had slipped out of the farmhouse through a window. Instead of causing a scene, he savored his victory. I think I could read his thoughts: *You see quite clearly that you have nowhere else to go other than here. I win.*

At first, life went on as if nothing happened, but the mirage didn't last very long. A few days later, a violent dispute ensued, with insults and punches showered upon us. The man seemed to be releasing all of the anger he had accumulated during our attempted escape. He hit my mother, and then he tried to tie a chain around her neck, like a dog, to prevent her from trying to escape again. Oh how I hated this barbarian. One of his brothers, who had come back to the farm, also rose to defend his family's honor. Using a broomstick, he started to beat the three of us. All we could do was take it.

To be honest, we never should have returned, despite the risk of being arrested in the countryside. Ever since our attempted escape, life at the farm had gone from just difficult to a true living hell. The family no longer trusted us, and they suspected that we were trying to escape at any given moment. The disagreements of the first few months descended into overt hostility. And my Chinese "stepfather" continued to demand that my mom give him a son. For the following weeks, we kept thinking about our failed attempt to escape, and we regretted our decision to come back. We started to think of new ways to flee, because our situation had become truly unbearable.

❖

Two months later, everything changed yet again: one morning, Mom approached me with a troubled look on her face.

"I think I'm pregnant," she whispered.

I was taken aback. With her "husband," she left for the nearest hospital to make sure. When she came back at the end of the day, she delivered the news: "I am indeed pregnant."

Our fate was sealed; we could no longer try to escape from the farm. We were forever bound to this barbaric peasant.

❖ 10

My mom was at a loss. For the first time in her life, she confided her deepest, most sensitive thoughts to me. I was thirteen years old, and she figured that by now I was old enough to understand the concerns of her adult world. On one hand, she was relieved because this baby would secure our future. Thanks to the baby, her husband would simmer down, and the family would finally begin to accept us. Perhaps one day, she hoped, we might even be able to obtain the residency permits that we so desperately needed. On the other hand, she was sad, because she had never wanted this baby. But either way, she knew for sure that she was going to have it.

She trusted this secret to me: "A long time ago, long before you were born, I went to see a fortune-teller.

He predicted that I would have two daughters and then a son."

I stayed silent. My mother's pregnancy was a turning point in our lives, but in the moment, I did not realize the extent of what it would bring. It might seem odd, but at that instant, I felt no emotion at all, and had no thoughts on the matter. I dispassionately analyzed the situation in relation to the only thing that mattered to me at the time: our survival. We were in an extremely vulnerable situation, and I did not have the heart to be introspective. I couldn't think about whether or not it was a good thing that my mother was about to bear this violent man's child. I simply thought about the risks of pregnancy for my mom and for us. My mom was already in her forties, so it was possible that the pregnancy might go badly. She might even lose her life. But, in case there were complications, how were we supposed to find medical assistance, there in the middle of nowhere? What would happen to Keumsun and me if she died during childbirth? These were the sorts of questions in my head. I was as emotionless as stone.

Another risk seemed more imminent. In case the police came, my mother would no longer be able to run away to hide in the forest like she used to. She would thus get arrested, and Keumsun and I would be left by ourselves at the mercy of the farmer. The day that I learned I would have a baby brother or sister, these were the kinds of thoughts that occupied me. It might seem selfish, but when you have to fight to survive, it's hard to be compassionate.

※

The fortune-teller turned out to be right. Mom had a baby boy. I will remember the day of his birth for the rest of my life. The four of us—Mom, the Chinese farmer, Keumsun, and I—were at the farm when she started having contractions.

The farmer wanted to bring my mom to the hospital where she had gotten her checkups done. Despite our illegal status, Mom hadn't had any problems because in that countryside hospital, they didn't ask to see papers as long as you paid the consultation fee. But on the day of the childbirth, my mom refused to leave the farm. The hospital was too far. She insisted that she'd be able to get by without medical help. After all, she had worked at a hospital in Eundeok, and had often helped her colleagues during childbirths. Besides, she had already given birth twice in her life and knew what to expect.

Keumsun and I hardly felt reassured, especially since there was no midwife and we would have to help with the delivery ourselves.

My mom explained to us that this was necessary. When she went into labor, I feared the worst. We disinfected scissors, using water that we boiled in the kettle above the fire in the kitchen. It was the only source of heat in the house. Then, along with Keumsun and my "stepfather," I pushed down on Mom's stomach. The baby wasn't coming out, and my mom was screaming at the top of her lungs. I was scared to death; I really thought she was about to die.

During her last checkup at the hospital, the doctors had expressed fear that the baby might not be in the correct position. But my mother, stubborn as is her nature, insisted that everything would be fine. In the end, the baby came out correctly. He had a big head and it was very wrinkly. Mom took the scissors from us and, without a hint of hesitation, cut the umbilical cord herself.

The man took the baby in his arms with pride. He had finally gotten what he wanted: a male descendent. Following Chinese tradition, he proudly hung red drapes over the front doors of the house to announce the new baby's birth to the neighborhood. Also according to tradition, for one hundred days, in order to shield against evil spirits and ailments, the mother and child could not go outside. Only the family was allowed to see the newborn during this time.

❖

The ambience at the farm was, for a short period after the birth of my baby brother, noticeably more relaxed. At first, I found the baby quite ugly, but I quickly became very fond of him. Chang Qian, his Chinese name, meant "brightness."

For the first few days, the baby's dad was filled with joy and was extremely proud of his son. Even his grandmother found him cute, and she began to show my mom, who was still bedridden, something akin to kindness. Keumsun and I started to feel a glimmer of hope. We thought we were finally about to be integrated into the family. The future seemed bright.

Of all of us in the family, I ended up becoming closest to the baby. That's because when spring arrived, Mom had to go back to the fields with Keumsun to work. Since I was the smallest and weakest, I was in charge of taking care of the baby during the day, as well as preparing meals for those who were working in the fields. Every morning I would play with the baby, feed him, and try to calm him whenever he cried. It was an onerous task, but I was happy to take it on.

However, it did mean that I was stuck inside while my friends played outside on the esplanade in front of the farm. I was sometimes split between my desire to have fun and my job as a babysitter. But I didn't mind. And if, miraculously, the baby stopped crying and started sleeping, I could go spend time with my friends. Never for too long though, because before noon, I had to make lunch for the entire family, all the while keeping an eye on the baby. Sometimes I was overwhelmed by the amount of work, but I didn't let that bother me terribly because I absolutely adored my baby brother ... even if he was the offspring of the man whom I hated so much.

❖

Alas, the peaceful family atmosphere was short-lived. The arguments and fights started flaring up again, just as they had before the child's birth. My "stepfather" was once again in a sour mood, and he took his anger out on us. However, we never did anything to provoke his anger. In reality, his resentment was directed toward his parents. He had hoped that the birth of his son would help him win the family inheritance. His younger brother was not about to accept defeat that easily, however. Ever since little Chang Qian was born, my "stepfather"'s younger brother had been living back on the farm with us. His objective was to prevent my "stepfather" from claiming the family inheritance. The brother sensed danger; the baby threatened his portion. And so he decided to return to the family farm to demonstrate to his parents his "filial piety." It was a meager inheritance, but it was better than nothing.

I had noticed that everyone in that family was very egotistical. Everyone, from the grandmother on down through each of the sons, thought only of his or her own personal and material interests. There was no solidarity in this family, no expression of true feeling.

In any case, my "stepfather" had to fight back if he wanted

to keep his new status in the family. His parents were not persuaded by my little brother's smiling little face. The grandma seemed to have a soft spot for her grandson, but of course that didn't do anything to change the patriarchal attitude in this region.

However, my mom's husband had high hopes and a lot of nerve. Shortly after Chang Qian's birth, he asked his mother for money to help him pay for the boy's education. He asked as though this would just be the first portion of his inheritance money. But his mother turned him down immediately.

"Why should I pay for your son's education?" she responded. "The child is yours, it's your responsibility."

He then burst out in anger, declaring, "Since you don't recognize him as your grandson, he is not my son either, and I will not take care of him!"

Then, to our horror, he took the baby and placed him dangerously on the wagon outside. It was winter and the temperature was bitterly cold. I was horrified. How could the man treat his own son like that? This incident reminded me of the awful nature we had seen time and again in this man. He only thought of himself. The only reason he had ever wanted a son was because he wanted his family's inheritance. He didn't love his son at all.

From that day forth, I started worrying constantly about my little brother's future. How would he become educated with such a father? I wanted to protect him; I felt like it was my responsibility as his older sister. Although I haven't seen him in many years now, I will never forget him.

After several months, the atmosphere on the farm became even worse because of the constant fighting between the man and his parents. Mom, Keumsun, and I had to clean up after them without uttering a word of complaint. We had no other option. With the arrival of the baby, trying to escape was no longer a viable option. Mom hadn't wanted the baby originally, but once she makes a decision, she sticks to it until the end. So our only option was to try to integrate ourselves into this family and make the best of things, at least for the time being.

And besides, at least at the farm we had food to eat. It was better to live miserably in China than to live on the brink of starvation in North Korea. This peasant family may have been poor, but at least they could provide food to fill our stomachs each day. A daily routine began to emerge. As much as possible, we attempted to keep to ourselves and stay out of the family's way. Each night, we snuggled together in the living room to watch TV shows. My Chinese began to improve. We all started to cheer up a little. And then in the evenings, I would fall asleep peacefully, in the complete silence of the countryside.

❖

Today, I realize that, in spite of everything we endured, we were nonetheless lucky. Like 70 percent of the thousands of women who cross the Chinese border each year, we had, unfortunately, fallen into the hands of human traffickers. But at least we had been spared the worst. Many other women who escape from North Korea face an even worse fate: forced prostitution in brothels and karaoke lounges. This also includes their children, even if the children are very young. These victims are scarred for life, and many feel ashamed of their pasts. As a result, even after managing to obtain freedom in South Korea, many of these women still suffer from great shame and live in the shadows.

❖

One night, at the end of winter 2002, we were watching TV when I fell asleep. Shortly after, my slumber was interrupted quite abruptly: someone was banging loudly on the front door. I understood right away what was happening. I rose as quickly as I could and dashed toward the back window to try to escape. It was too late. The blinding white lights already clouded my vision. We were trapped.

My mom's husband looked frightened. He opened the door. A plainclothes policeman appeared and, toward Mom, Keumsun, and me, he barked: "Pack your belongings and come with me!"

There was a car waiting for us outside. It was the Chinese

police. The officers instructed the three of us to get in the car. My heart was pounding. I was so scared that, for a moment, I completely forgot about my little brother. I was so focused on the situation at hand that I didn't even realize that I might never see him again. With the police present, the farmer didn't dare say anything and just stood there, holding on tightly to his son.

The man couldn't put up a fight because he knew what he had been doing was illegal. He did not have the right to marry a North Korean, nor did he have the right to provide housing for us. He risked being arrested as well. And so it was everyone for him or herself. Someone must have denounced us.

Normally, the neighbors warned us in advance whenever a suspicious car rolled by. But this time the police had come in the middle of the night, with the headlights off, in an ordinary car. The dogs didn't even make noise when they arrived.

Soon we found ourselves at the small police station in this town. There, we tried to appeal to the officers' humanity.

"I have a baby here. I am married to a Chinese man," explained my mother.

They didn't listen to her and locked the three of us in the restroom, since the station was too small to even have jail cells.

In the restroom, there was a window with steel bars,

through which we could see the street. We started imagining ways to escape. The bars didn't look that firmly attached to the wall. With a bit of effort and a few hours' time, we might have been able break them off the wall. Since we were so small, we could easily slip through in the middle of the night without being seen. But my mother said we should just forget it, because the plan was too risky and could potentially land us in even more trouble, if we were caught.

She was hoping instead that her husband would buy our freedom by bribing the police, which happened often in this area. But that hope was in vain: that horrible man did nothing to help release us from jail. Never mind that he'd made us work in the fields like slaves, and that my mom had given him the child that he so desperately wanted—a child that he treated poorly but kept nonetheless. I didn't know whether I was more overcome by anger or by sorrow.

The next day, we were once again sent by car to an unknown location.

As we were driving, I began to understand exactly where we were heading.

❖

The car stopped in front of a building surrounded by guards in uniform. They threw us in a jail cell full of North Korean women. Like us, they were waiting to be sent back to their home country. Rumors were circling about. We heard that those who escaped to China were sent back to North Korea with iron rings around their necks. Were they going to torture us? The guards were heartless. One woman who tried to bribe a guard with cash was struck savagely across the face. Among the detainees, talking was strictly forbidden. On the other side, I heard yelling coming from the men's cell. I started to hate the Chinese. I was afraid, I was in pain, and I couldn't stop thinking about my little brother, whom we'd left behind. My heart broke at the thought of him. I thought that we had made a terrible mistake by not escaping through the restroom window at the police station. But now, it was too late.

After four days of this nightmare, the guards let us out, with our hands cuffed behind our backs, and then pushed us on a bus, our wrists torn. The curtains were drawn, but I peeked through them and saw little snippets of the countryside as we drove. Soon the mountains disappeared and we saw a river. We were driving across a bridge. I recognized the landmarks. We were at the Tumen River, the border between North Korea and China. The date was March 31, 2002, and we were on our way back to North Korea.

11

Take off your clothes!"
Under the blinding white light, I took off my tattered clothing piece by piece.

"Bend over!" shouted the officer.

I was completely naked and being subjected to humiliating torment. I bent my knees, crouched down, and then got back up again. I did this repeatedly until I was out of breath. Nothing was to be hidden, not even the most intimate areas of our bodies. After making her way through this group of naked women, a female officer in uniform grabbed me extremely hard. She shone a flashlight in my ears and then in my mouth. She inspected my teeth and then reached behind my gums. She dragged her hand down my chest. I started to shudder. Then her hand reached my stomach. She didn't stop there: a little farther down and she continued to search my body by pushing her fingers inside me. I clenched my jaw. Everything had to be removed, even tampons.

❖

Mom and Keumsun were subjected to the same degrading treatment. It was what everyone who escaped from North Korea and got sent back had to go through.

"When did you betray your country, you fucking cunt? With who? Where did you go, you worthless piece of shit?" screamed the interrogating officer.

The violent and abusive interrogation continued. I didn't answer his questions. That only infuriated him all the more.

Then I was thrown into a cell where some sixty other women were already crammed like cattle. The cell was tiny and was hardly built to fit sixty people. On one side, there were steel bars preventing us from escaping. On the other side, there was a simple hole in the ground where we could go to the bathroom, right in front of everyone. There wasn't enough space to lie down or stretch. At night, we slept next to one another, with each person's head against someone else's chest. It was impossible, however, to sleep for very long. In the middle of the night, my little brother appeared to me in a terrible nightmare. In my nightmare, he screamed as he was being boiled alive in a pot of water. He was just fourteen months old when I left him. What would happen to him at the hands of his inhumane father?

That night, for the first time in my life, I began to feel anger toward my country. Up until then, I'd never felt any hatred toward North Korea. We only left for China in order to survive, because we didn't have any food. We didn't have anything against Kim Jong-il, nor did we have anything against the system—we were apolitical. But in that prison, for the first time, my eyes were opened to the horrors perpetrated by the Kim regime, and I felt my anger begin to build.

❖

Only once, when I was very little, had I already started feeling the seeds of doubt about our country. One morning in primary school, the teacher told us that we would attend an important event in our education: the execution of a man who was guilty of committing "serious crimes." The playground started to fill with commotion.

"I know who is going to be killed! It's your father!" taunted some of the meaner boys. I stayed quiet, worrying silently.

Before lunch, the teachers took us downtown in order of rank. The crowd gathered near an empty lot, right next to the bridge. Since we were little, we were positioned on top of the bridge so that we could have a clearer view of what was happening, so that we wouldn't miss this important pedagogical lesson. Some privilege that was.

Then a car with heavily tinted windows appeared. Policemen dragged out several men whose heads and faces were covered with headscarves. The crowd started to shiver. After one final symbolic interrogation, the accused men pitifully admitted their wrongdoings. Afterward, they were tied to wooden poles planted along the river. I didn't understand how they managed to remain so emotionless when they knew they were about to die.

And then suddenly, we heard a deafening noise. I jumped, startled. The gunshots seemed to last an eternity. After a while, all was quiet again. Through the plume of smoke that was dissipating into the air, I could make out gigantic puddles of blood, littered with pieces of flesh mixed with a white liquid. It was there that I learned to feel compassion for others; I felt an immense outpouring of pity, a feeling of fraternity toward these men who had been slaughtered so heartlessly.

I was wondering what would happen to their remains—the last vestiges of their existence—when all of a sudden a strange-looking man emerged from the crowd and started sniffing the shredded pieces of bodies. Such was the nature of a hungry animal. He took the gray, gelatinous pieces of flesh and looked at them hungrily before devouring them in front of everyone. I was terrified. We were told that this crazy man thought that eating a human brain would cure him of his maladies.

As everyone left to get lunch, I stood still, horrified.

After this first terrible ordeal, I became used to these public executions, which were a routine occurrence. Even so, each time, I still had my qualms. I remember a man who was sent to the execution pole for having "insulted our Great Leader" Kim Il-sung. His crime? He had snatched some bronze letters off an official inscription of our Great Leader. No doubt the man had just hoped to ameliorate his living conditions during the famine by selling the metal to the Chinese for a bit of cash. It was a crime punishable by death. When I heard the shots being fired, I felt that I was witnessing a great injustice.

It's just bronze. It's not fair to die just for a bit of bronze, I thought to myself. For the first time, I was revolted. But I kept all these thoughts to myself, because I knew that I would have been seen in a very bad light by my classmates and teachers if I had vocalized these opinions. In North Korea, everyone kept tabs on his or her neighbors. Even among friends, people could not be trusted. Starting from a young age, I noticed that my parents agreed with things publicly that were quite different from what they said at home. One day, a group of men were executed for stealing rice from the army reserves. After the execution, my parents commended the men's courage.

But only after our front doors were firmly shut.

❖

All of these memories came back to me while I was ruminating in that nauseating North Korean cell, from which we would soon be taken out for one last interrogation.

There was no delay in giving us the verdict: as we had all betrayed Kim Jong-il and the tenets of socialism, we had to be "reeducated" before being sent to prison.

Thus, one morning, handcuffed and escorted by guards, we left to cross the countryside, by foot, until we reached the reeducation camp. Once we were inside, we were finally relieved of our handcuffs, but the relief was short-lived. We found ourselves in the middle of an immense esplanade, surrounded by a chain-link fence, with some barracks in the middle where we would be tossed to spend each night. The men lay against one side, the women against the other. But we could never sleep for long. We were there to work for the state. It was part of our "socialist reeducation," an intermediate step before we were to be sent to prison in my hometown of Eundeok.

❖

From dawn until dusk, Keumsun and Mom worked the fields. I, alongside the other children and adolescents in the camp, cleaned the barracks, sorted the corn kernels and protected them from the rats that prowled around. Then at night, we had to attend daily brainwashing sessions. Seated in a circle, we read out loud from the works of Kim Il-sung and Kim Jong-il. We would mindlessly repeat them until we had them memorized. For twenty-five days, we followed the same ritual, which was always exhausting, especially when our stomachs were empty. We were barely fed anything... once again, I was hungry.

❖

One morning, the guards came to take us to Chongjin like we were livestock. There, we would be transferred to the Eundeok prison. Back to where we came from. It was so humiliating to be sent to my grandparents' hometown like we were dirty criminals. How were they going to treat us in this prison? Here we were again, nearly four years after we'd first left, and this time returning as criminals, guilty of committing "grave crimes." We knew what sort of penalties were reserved for those kinds of criminals. Even if it seems crazy, given that we had just been captured from China and that we'd suffered so much abuse while we were there, Mom had only one idea in mind: we had to get out of North Korea again.

Alas, it seemed that now, our chances of escaping had been reduced to almost none.

❖

And it was then and there that fate gave us a little break, just when we least expected it. A man was sent from Eundeok to escort other prisoners from the same district. At the last minute, the administration realized that we were also from that district, and they decided to add us to the convoy. The man was reluctant, but we convinced him that he had no other choice. The Chongjin prison authorities were eager to get rid of these inmates that they had to monitor, and for whom daily rations of food were an extra burden. The food shortage was so severe that even the policemen and junior military men put their own survival above all else.

Surely, we knew, our escort wouldn't want to share with us his already low supply of provisions. And so, after we had just left the reeducation camp, we exploited the situation. Mom proposed a deal with the man in charge of escorting us: we would travel to Eundeok through our own means, so he wouldn't have to take care of the costs of transporting us or feeding us. Since we had been added to the convoy at the last minute, there were no documents listing our names that obligated our escort to hand us over to the authorities—he wouldn't be taking any risk by letting us go. After a few minutes of persuasion, he agreed, and we were free!

It was a miracle.

But what were we going to do with this fleeting newfound freedom? Between our homeland and us, a link had been broken forever. We had no money, and we were, under the eyes of the law, considered criminals, fugitives even.

We didn't hesitate about our destination, not even for a moment. We refused to be considered exiles in our own country. The only thing we had in mind: flee, once more, to China, despite all the risks.

* 12

Through the windows, I watched as the Chinese countryside passed before my eyes. On the seat of the taxi,
Mom was worrying herself sick. We didn't have even one
penny to our names, but we told the driver that we would
pay him when we arrived at our destination. When we began passing through more familiar landscape, my mom
started to tense up. Had we turned completely crazy? In a
few minutes, we would be back with the man whom we hated
so much. Although we really didn't have any better options,
we feared that we might have been jumping out of the fry-
ing pan and into the fire.

Keumsun was against returning to the Chinese farmer.
In fact, I was the one who had convinced my mother to do
so. To be honest, it was mostly because I wanted to see my

little brother again, no matter what the price was. I missed him so much that he had started appearing in my dreams. And I was so worried for his future, at the hands of that unscrupulous Chinese peasant. Out of the three of us, I was the closest to him. While my mother and Keumsun worked in the fields around the farm, I, deemed still too frail for the hard work of agriculture, had taken care of him. I loved him, and the knowledge that I was going to see him again consoled me despite the somber reality of the future that was waiting for us on the farm.

❖

Admittedly, we no longer knew where else we could go. Ever since our fortuitous escape in Chongjin a few weeks ago, we had been on the run, and owing to our status as fugitives, we were exhausted. Immediately after our liberation, we went straight north, toward the border, while laying low. Always we moved with only one goal in mind: to leave our homeland forever. The situation in North Korea had gotten so bad that our modest clothes made in China were worth a fortune there. We sold them, and with the bit of cash this brought us we were able to feed ourselves for three days. Then, with nothing left to lose, we headed toward the border.

Groping around in the dark, we found the path at the Tumen River, by now very familiar to us. But this time, luck was not on our side.

While we were preparing to cross the river, a border patrolman appeared. He brought us to the border patrol station for questioning, and then the next day we were transferred to a nearby military base for an even more intensive questioning.

"Did you go to China?" the soldier asked.

"No, I just went to do some business near the river, that's all."

I was lying and he didn't believe me for a second.

"Do you have any money? Where did you come from?" the soldier wanted to know.

I didn't answer. I was by then used to these interrogations and could handle myself well. He was insistent, but at least he was polite, which I appreciated.

And then we heard the verdict: we were going to be sent back to the labor camp where we had been taken a few weeks ago, when we had first been arrested.

After hearing the news, I felt hopeless. As soon as we left the base, Mom and Keumsun fell to the floor crying and refused to move an inch. I felt a little embarrassed, because I could tell they were trying to gain the pity of the officer, and I didn't think it stood a chance of working.

But somehow it did. The man sympathized with our plight, but he didn't seem to know what to do with us. Finally, after a long moment of hesitation, he told us that we could leave. With our feeble bodies and tattered rags for clothing, he must have thought that we would never be able to make it to China . . . but he was wrong.

❖

That same night, we tried once more to cross the Tumen. Again, a border patrolman found us. In a panic, I ran to go hide in a nearby barn. To no avail: the policeman found me shortly after. Again, we repeated the same scenario. We spent the night at the station and then, the next day, we were transferred to the military base, where we were found ourselves face-to-face with the same officer yet again. Remembering us, he didn't even bother interrogating us anymore, and he even gave us two pieces of candy. Then he let us escape again, warning us that we should be more discreet this time around.

That policeman showed himself to be compassionate. Since our first escape four years earlier, the number of people trying to flee from North Korea had increased significantly. In response, the regime had also increased the number of patrolmen along the border, but they didn't know what to do with all of their miserable prisoners.

At eleven that night, we trudged through the freezing waters of the Tumen. Luckily, this time, no one came to bother us. In a few minutes, we reached the other side and were in China once again. Immediately, we bolted deep into the countryside, to get as far away as possible from the border. But, in the time since our first contact with the local population and our first stay in China, I understood that the atmosphere had changed quite a bit. At that time, the local residents offered us food and advice. However, as the number of North Korean escapees had been increasing, they stole from the farms, and the towns along the borders began to deteriorate. Now, no one trusted one another anymore, and we were without many options.

❖

After three days of aimless wandering, we were still penniless and living on empty stomachs. And so it appeared that going back to the farm of my mom's "husband," at least temporarily, was the lesser of two evils. The idea of seeing that awful man again repulsed us but it was, for the moment, the only way we could survive. After one final moment of hesitation, we jumped into a taxi.

A few hours later, we pulled up on the main street of the village that we had left less than two months ago. Through the glass, I recognized the houses, and then the taxi approached the side that led toward the farm.

I held conflicting emotions within me. On one hand, I was afraid of seeing the farmer and his family again, the family that had treated us so poorly. But on the other hand, my heart skipped a beat whenever I thought about seeing my brother again. How was he faring? I feared the worst.

When we finally reached the esplanade in front of the farm, my Chinese "cousins," the farmer's nephew and niece, were the first ones to spot the car. They screamed in joy when they saw us through the windows. They looked so happy to see their two playmates again: Keumsun and me! This warmed my heart to see.

The farmer, alerted by the commotion, showed up at the entrance of the farm. He was flabbergasted at the sight of us. He could hardly believe his eyes and a big grin appeared on his face. For once, he seemed happy to see us. I got the impression that he never thought he'd see us again. He happily paid the taxi driver and even left a generous tip. Originally, we had offered the taxi driver eighty yuan for the ride, but the farmer gave him a hundred instead. It seemed as if he had really missed us, and that he was genuinely happy to have us back. But I knew it was just a mirage. For him, our return meant that he now had three sets of arms to exploit. And for a lonely man, it was always better to have a woman by his side.

I hardly spent any time dwelling on those thoughts. The only thing that mattered for me was to give my little brother a great big hug. I found him inside the farm. To my relief, he looked well. I felt tears run down my cheeks when I caught sight of him. His cheeks and his stomach were plump and he looked healthy and well fed. His skin was very tan, which we weren't terribly happy to see, because Koreans think that light skin is a sign of beauty. But it hardly mattered, because he was smiling.

❖

Even though we were back, it was impossible to live again on the farm as if nothing had happened. We had to change our survival tactics in China. A denunciation was almost certainly the reason behind our arrest. The police now recognized us and knew who we were, and if they found out we were back they wouldn't hesitate to arrest us again. The farm was no longer a safe place for us. But where could we go instead?

As was her nature, Keumsun was the first to take the initiative. She wanted to go live in the city. I was a bit more cautious, as well as younger, and thus not as willing to take the same risks. Her decision stemmed largely from the attraction of living in the city: she had just turned eighteen and discovered the guilty pleasures of adult life. In this village, eighteen was the age that a woman typically got married. Our neighbors soon started to try finding husbands for each of us. They wanted to introduce Keumsun to suitors. They organized blind dates for her. At first, Keumsun refused. But, at the insistence of her friends and cousins, she finally agreed to go on one of these dates. She didn't like the man she was matched with at all. Moreover, she had no intention of getting married at this age. Eighteen years old was far too young. She wanted to build a life for herself first.

To distance herself from the pressure she faced in the village, she landed a babysitting job in Sukhyun-Jin, a town that was at least an hour away from the farm. For her, it was the beginning of a new life, one of independence. She started to earn her own money. Some weekends when she returned to the farm, she would bring little gifts and cigarettes for the family. Later she would go work in another small city, Yongil, as a waitress in a restaurant, where the boss would exploit her illegal status. Nevertheless, living in the city was less risky than living in the countryside, because it was easier to stay anonymous among the crowded population. Moreover, it was a good idea for Keumsun and me to be separated now that we were adults. At least now, if the police came to take us, we could not be taken together.

For about six months, I keep myself busy at the farm by taking care of my brother and managing the household. I also started to make a bit of money. I often left to go to the forest and collect mushrooms and medicinal herbs that I would sell in the village whenever wholesalers came from the city. These herbs were critical in traditional Chinese medicine, and they are often very expensive. Sometimes I went fishing with my friends at the river, so that we could sell the fish for a profit. I couldn't always go to school, but I still learned many things. There, you had to be proactive if you wanted to survive. And in China, if you had the determination and entrepreneurial spirit, you could go out and make money.

❖

During the winter of 2002, six months after she left for the city, Keumsun asked me whether I wanted to come join her. She had found a job for me in a bakery in Won Chin, a city next to where she lived. I was sixteen, and I was nervous about leaving my mom for the first time, but I had to learn how to take care of myself. And so I accepted her offer.

There, I learned about the harsh reality of working in a business. I slept no more than five hours a night, in a little dorm situated on the fourth floor above the bakery. I helped bake the cakes very early in the morning. The bakery opened at eight a.m. each morning, but my workday began at five every morning with the others. My primary task was to break open the eggs and separate the yolks from the whites, and to supervise the baking. After the bakery closed, we had to clean the shop until late into the night. I didn't get to see sunlight in that workshop, and I was exhausted from the sleep deprivation. Several times, I fell asleep on the job, forgetting the cakes in the oven and causing them to burn. I began setting an alarm to ensure that I would wake up before the cakes were done baking, thereby avoiding catastrophe.

This lifestyle was even harder on me because I was so far from my mom, but I held on. And at least I got to eat a lot of cakes. I quickly gained a lot of weight and actually became quite chubby. I weighed in at around 115 pounds—a record for me. Especially when you consider that more than once, I had nearly died of hunger. But I wasn't happy. Koreans think that you have to be thin if you want to be pretty. I didn't feel pretty anymore; I didn't feel comfortable in my own skin.

At the bakery, no one knew that I was a North Korean living in China illegally, and owing to my ability to speak Chinese, I was able to hide my true identity. My boss might have suspected something, but he never said anything and had no problem paying me each month in cash. He never asked me for a residency permit. The first month, I made about three hundred yuan (about thirty-five dollars). My salary may have been modest, but at least I finally had a real job. I was so proud of myself. What's more, for each of the following months, I received a raise of fifty yuan each month. At the end of six months, I had a monthly salary of six hundred yuan (about seventy dollars). But my employer took fifty yuan each month from my salary as a deposit that he said he'd give back to me in a year, if I were still working there. He didn't want his employees to quit and work for one of his competitors after just a few months, after having been trained by him, which happens quite often in China.

During that time, my mom didn't leave the farm for fear of being arrested. She often slept on the roof or in the mountains from fear of a denunciation. Worse, her relationship with our "in-laws" deteriorated, and the disputes flared up again. Her "husband" always suspected that my mom would try to flee with my little brother, and so he watched her constantly. Whenever I came to visit the farm, he forbade us from sleeping in the same room as my little brother. But my mom hung on. She wanted to stay near her son, despite the fighting and her constant fear of getting arrested.

❖

Throughout the course of several months, I began to feel more and more comfortable at the bakery. But at the start of summer 2003, a new turn of events derailed the life I was building. One day, I was told to go to the counter in the bakery. There was a phone call for me. My heart started pounding in worry.

"I couldn't take it anymore. I left the farm. I couldn't stand that life anymore," my mother informed me, with a hint of guilt in her voice.

She had had to leave her son behind her. She couldn't handle the increasing number of police raids anymore. Each time, she had to crawl on all four limbs to the hills. She had to spend many nights alone on the roof, fighting off insects. She told me that her back was completely red, after having been bitten by so many bugs. And so one day she fled the farm without revealing her plan to anyone. She left on foot and then took a bus. She had since started working on another farm as a housemaid. She cooked and worked in the fields. She wasn't paid, but in exchange she was given housing by this new family, who treated her much better than her "husband" ever had.

I was very surprised by her call and could not help but let my thoughts drift to my little brother, still alone at the farm, under the cruel hands of his father. But at the same time, I felt sympathy for my mother, and I completely understood her decision.

❖

A few days after this call, my boss came to find me in the shop.

"You have a visitor. Your stepfather is looking for you at the counter."

I was petrified. Trying to remain calmer than I felt, I asked my boss to tell him that I wasn't here today. He agreed, without asking me any questions.

But three or four days later, the farmer came back again. He was undoubtedly trying to find my mother through any means he could. I managed to avoid him again, but I knew that he would not leave me alone and that he was ready to do whatever was necessary to get his hands on me. I knew that I was in danger. And so I left. I couldn't stay there. I had to change my location. Without giving him any details, I told my boss that I had to quit. I had worked less than a year at the bakery, so I wasn't able to get back the fifty monthly yuan that had been taken as a deposit during my training. But in any case, I didn't have a choice. Luckily, my boss still let me stay on the fourth floor while I looked for other options.

My decision was well-timed, too, because the farmer never stopped trying to get ahold of me. Near the end of September, I received a panicked call from Keumsun. She told me that she had been taken hostage by our "stepfather." The day was September 21, my mom's birthday. Keumsun still worked as a waitress in Yongil, but without a phone number where we could reach her, we had not yet been able to update her on Mom's recent escape. And so Keumsun had wanted to surprise our mother by returning to the farm to celebrate her birthday. When she got there, the man immediately saw an opportunity for blackmail, or at least a way to find my mother, and so he held her there. She had to wait for night to fall before she could escape.

My sister was at a loss and didn't want to go back to her job at Yongil. Her objective was to get as far away as possible from this accursed farmer as quickly as possible, and to leave the countryside and this border region where the police swarmed in search of North Koreans.

"Let's go to Dalian. It's a large city, and we'll have more opportunities to find work and less risk of getting arrested," Keumsun said.

I got into contact with my mom again, and we persuaded her to leave with us to head south, to Dalian. It's the largest metropolis in the region, and an entirely different environment waited for us there. I was hoping that this new environment would be a change for the better.

✦

At the end of September, the three of us were finally reunited in Yongil, and we took the bus toward Dalian and its six million residents. We didn't know anyone there. When we arrived, we spent two nights in a shabby hotel near the bus station. And then we discovered a help center for the unemployed where we stayed, and we started looking for work right away.

For four months, I would take up little jobs: handing out flyers, cleaning, cooking. Keumsun found a job as a waitress in a Korean restaurant. Mom was hired by an old, bedridden couple. The old man was essentially unable to leave his bed, so she had to take care of him all the time, washing him and caring for his needs. But it was a stable, full-time job. All of this let us save up money. At the beginning of 2004, I had made three thousand yuan (about three hundred and fifty dollars). While we were working hard, we felt safer and more secure. We could, once again, start planning for our future.

Keumsun, as usual, had grand ideas in mind, including some very specific plans. She proposed that we go farther south, to Shanghai, the economic capital of the country. She was bored at the restaurant and thought that there were few opportunities for her in Dalian. She was ambitious and wanted to try her luck in that immense, rapidly developing metropolis. And when Keumsun has an idea, it's impossible to change her mind.

My mother was not quite ready to leave Dalian. But Keumsun had no qualms, and she decided to go alone. I wanted to stay near my mom. Moreover, I didn't feel ready to take that step yet. I gave eighty yuan to my sister to help finance her journey, and we let her go to Shanghai. Maybe we would join her later.

The real reason my mom didn't want to travel too much farther was because she wanted to see her son again. The Chinese New Year was coming up soon, and she dreamed of returning to the farm to make a surprise visit. We had accumulated a decent amount of money working in Dalian:

more than three thousand yuan. It was a lot for us. It boosted our morale and gave us the idea that celebrating New Year's "as a family" might be possible. A crazy idea, perhaps, but I really wanted to see my little brother. Mom thought that with this money, we would be able to buy groceries and even patch together a little party at the farm. As for me, I just wanted to spend a few days spoiling my little brother.

This idea would soon show itself to be one of the worst mistakes we made during our journey. We acted from the heart rather than from the head.

❖

Two days before the Chinese New Year, we traveled unannounced to the farm, surprising the farmer and his family. We explained that we had made some money and come back to celebrate New Year's with them. We were sincere: despite all the abuse and the drama we had suffered at their hands, the people on this farm were the closest thing to family we had in this country. And at any rate, there was now a baby that tied us all together forever.

But in the main room where everyone was reunited, my little brother was nowhere to be found.

The farmer was surprised to see us; he didn't know what to say. He seemed to waffle between relief and anger. He didn't turn us down, but right next to him, there was a man who was going to ruin everything. It was one of the farmer's younger brothers, a delinquent whom we had rarely seen at the farm. Because he was a thief, he often had run-ins with the police. And now he immediately saw an opportunity to exploit this situation. He told us that we would not see our baby unless we first handed over some of our money to him. It was blatant blackmail.

We were crushed. We had come here with good intentions, to spend some happy times together, to reconcile. But there was no way we would give in to this blackmail. The first night, we tried to stay calm, hoping that the atmosphere at the farm would improve after a few hours. We slept in the big room. The next morning, my mom tried to take the lead and asked her "husband" directly about the reasons behind the blackmail. His defense was weak at best. And just when it seemed like he was about to lower his guard, his younger brother appeared and showed himself to be unrelenting.

Hours went by, and my little brother was still nowhere to be seen. We became angrier and angrier. We felt betrayed.

And that's when the storm broke. There was yelling everywhere. Mom decided that enough was enough. We would be better off leaving immediately. We would have to miss our chance to see the child; they had left us no choice. Unhesitatingly, she stood up and pulled me toward the front door. It was already dark outside. We walked through the night along the esplanade, with no intention of returning. But suddenly, our "uncle" caught up to us and tried to block us from leaving. The farmer seized our backpacks and carried them back to his house. He wanted our money; it was all they cared about. We fought and fought and argued until we finally managed to escape again. The farmer didn't follow us. He was convinced that by snatching our backpacks, he had taken possession of our money. What he didn't know was that my mom had hidden the money behind her belt. There was no going back for us now.

We ran as fast as we could along the road that led toward the village. The ground was slippery because of all the snow and ice. It was the middle of January, bitterly cold out, and the ground was covered in a thick blanket of snow. But no matter, we did not have a minute to lose. As soon as the farmer and his brother realized our bags held no money, they would come chasing after us. We had to get off the road so that we could obscure our path. And so we ran across the fields, through the pitch-blackness of the night. Even though the snow was up to my knees, I continued at a dead run until I could no longer breathe. We had left in such a rush that I didn't even have the time to put on my shoes. I was still wearing my slippers. But there was not a moment to lose. We had to get as far away as possible from that godforsaken farm. We forced ourselves to move forward, right up until dawn.

This is how we celebrated Chinese New Year 2004. What a nightmare. At that time, I didn't yet know that I had set foot on the farm for the last time in my life.

In the early morning, after our mad dash through the white countryside, we finally found a bus stop next to the road. We headed toward the village where the bakery I used to work at was located. There, I bought some warm clothes and shoes. We found a run-down hotel, which cost five yuan (less than a dollar) per night, where we could rest a little.

It was the worst New Year's of my life.

❖ 13

I felt more depressed than ever before. In line with Chinese
tradition, firecrackers flared all around us. The whole village was celebrating. We felt lonely and discouraged. It had
been six and a half years since I stopped going to school. I
had neither prospects for the future nor a house to live in.
Worst of all, we had left my little brother behind, possibly
forever. I missed him terribly and thought of him often. It
was during those instants where I felt a pure hatred toward
my "stepdad." Sometimes he made me hate him so much
that I just wanted to kill him with my own two hands.

❖

The next day, we took the bus toward Dalian. Mom returned
right away to the old couple she had worked for. They still

needed her help, since the old man's condition was deteriorating. And so she got back to work immediately. But I had
already had enough of this city. I wanted to get as far away
as possible, I felt stifled there. Keumsun had left us a cell
phone number. I called her from a phone booth.

"I'm coming to Shanghai. I can't stand it here anymore."

One week after my return to Dalian, I was on my way
again, headed south. I left my mom behind, and I hoped
that in this strange and mysterious new city a new, more
pleasant chapter would unfold in my life.

After reaching the Shanghai station, I follow Keumsun's
instructions to find her at her workplace. This city was nothing like Dalian. It was a labyrinth that felt even more immense, with narrow streets swarming with people, and it
was very dirty. Finally, I found myself in front of a Korean
supermarket. It was there that Keumsun had found a job
as a cashier. She worked so hard that she didn't even have
time to come pick me up at the station. But I was extremely
happy to see her again. After a few minutes of catching up,
I realized that she was getting along quite well here, and
she shared a room with a coworker.

Later, when the store was a little less hectic, Keumsun
told me she had had a hard time at first, when she got here,
without any friends or family with her. She did not have
enough money to survive without a job. With no better options, she spent several nights sleeping at the station like a

hobo. But here there were opportunities for employment if you were willing to look for them. She gave me tips on how to find a job here as well. The first step was to obtain some fake papers for myself. To my great surprise, I discovered that nothing was easier than forging identification in this city. There were flyers everywhere advertising fake IDs for a mere hundred yuan (less than fifteen dollars). All you had to do was call the number on the flyer, bring a photo—and of course some money—and before you knew it, you had a fake residency permit. At the time, ID cards were very rudimentary and it was quite easy to fake them.

In Shanghai, a residency permit, even if it was a fake, opened doors. I quickly landed myself a job as a waitress in a restaurant run by South Koreans. My working conditions were much better than they had been at the bakery, and my coworkers were very nice to me. Little by little, I started to find my niche within the city, largely thanks to my sister.

But one day, four months after I arrived, Keumsun looked simultaneously excited and rueful. She told me, "Mom called. She tried to go back to the farm again, to see Chang Qian . . . but it went badly. She wants to come join us."

And so we were all once more reunited. My mother also obtained some false papers when she got here, and the three of us moved together into a room.

❖

In the anonymity of this city in the middle of an economic boom, we started a new life. Keumsun was the first one to be able to take care of herself. She even fell in love with a Chinese boy. I wasn't quite that at ease here just yet, but I became acquainted with the culture of South Korea thanks to my work in the restaurant. It was my first time making contact with our "enemies" to the south, and it went rather well. They spoke Korean with a different accent, but they ate the same things we do. We could understand each other. Growing up, I was taught in school that South Korea was "the puppet regime of the imperialist Americans," and that it was preparing to invade us at any moment. In Shanghai, for the first time, I was able to form my own opinions. I started to watch South Korean television shows. Over time, I became a fan of South Korean dramas, discovered K-pop, and even became a fan of artists who have become stars in China. I will remember forever the first CD I ever bought.

Our material living conditions were also steadily growing better and better. My mother too found a job of her own. She started working as a housemaid again, this time for two South Korean expatriates who shared a big house. They were very generous and rather pleased to find an employee who spoke their language. There, Mom made eighteen hundred yuan per month, just a bit over two hundred dollars—not bad at all. Whenever they left to go back to South Korea during their vacations, her bosses gave us the keys so that we could stay at their place. What luxury! Especially in comparison to the slums that we had been living in for seven years. One day, the day before the *Seollal*, the Korean New Year, they even gave us a hundred-dollar bill before boarding the plane for South Korea.

❖

Little by little, I started to dream about going to South Korea. In Shanghai, thanks to the South Koreans who treated us so nicely, I rediscovered my roots, my native language, and formed a clearer picture of the world. But I couldn't study, nor hope to find a good job, as long I was here illegally. I didn't want to be an illegal resident, or to live with fake identification, for the rest of my life. Here, we still lived in constant fear of getting arrested. In South Korea, I would finally be able to live my life in the open. Maybe I could even start going to school again. I learned that in South Korea, the government granted South Korean citizenship to all escapees from North Korea, as long as you could prove that you weren't a spy.

The only issue was getting there. The Chinese police closely monitor the South Korean embassy and consulates. It was impossible to go through that route. The only thing we could do was travel through another country to get to our promised land. But how could we do that without passports?

❖

Eventually, we learned that there were smuggling rings that could get people to South Korea. But you had to pay, and pay a lot. And how were we to make contact with any of these smugglers?

A friend and colleague of ours clandestinely gave us the phone number of a smuggler. In 2006, summoning up all my courage, I called this mysterious number. A brusque masculine voice answered. It told me the conditions of the deal: twenty thousand yuan (almost twenty-five hundred dollars) per head, to be paid in cash in China, and then the same to be paid by credit card once we made it to Seoul. It was a huge sum of money for us. I asked him for details.

"Where will we pass through? Is it dangerous? Are we sure to arrive at the right place?"

The questions just flowed from my mouth. But the man was not very talkative and did not want to engage in conversation. He obviously didn't want to stay on the line any longer than absolutely necessary. His answers were very vague. The only thing he was clear about was the price. However, he added that in a few days, one group would be leaving and that if we wanted to join them, we had to make a decision soon. Very, very soon.

I hung up, troubled.

For this offer, the options were either to take it or leave it, with little information and no guarantee of success. And all the risks involved were ours.

For three days, we thought things through. Were we ready to risk everything again? To hit the road once again and give up the comfort that we had finally been able to enjoy for two years in Shanghai? Did we still dare to run the risk of getting arrested at the border and then getting sent back to the hell that is North Korea? Furthermore, the smuggler had seemed a bit sketchy. When we talked to him again on the phone, he asked us for even more money.

Keumsun was hesitant. She decided to remain in China. She did not want to be separated from her boyfriend.

❖

But this time, I was determined. I decided that I was going to leave and hope for better things in South Korea. And seeing how determined I was, my mom decided to come with me. Maybe she just didn't want me to go alone. It was an all or nothing decision. The year was 2006, and it had been nine years that we had been wandering all over. My mom and I did not want to spend the rest of our lives trembling at the idea of getting arrested and once again being sent back to a country that wasn't exactly going to welcome us with open arms. We wanted to have a future, a real future. So we saved up as much money as we could, and told the smuggler that we would accept his deal. I told my boss that I had to quit my waitress job, without giving him any details, and he didn't ask for any. I think he understood the situation.

Over the phone, the smuggler left me private instructions: make your way to the Mongolian border, where you will meet us.

It was the last step before reaching paradise ... or another living hell.

❖ 14

After getting off the bus, I called the smuggler to let him know we were there, just as we had arranged beforehand. In the crowd of the Erenhot bus station, we anxiously waited for our liberator. I still had my qualms. We were in a small town near the border in a Chinese province called Inner Mongolia. It felt like we were in the middle of nowhere. This province adjoins the neighboring country of Mongolia, an independent nation that fought for centuries against China. It was through this country that we had to escape, according to the explanations given to us on the phone. We were at the mercy of many people: the border guards, the Chinese police, and even this smuggler, whom I still wasn't sure I completely trusted.

Mom and I had just traveled through half of China with

our savings hidden in our clothing and with fear in our hearts. We had first boarded the train toward Beijing, then gotten on a bus heading northwest toward the Mongolian border.

Erenhot is the last Chinese city on the route toward Ulan Bator, the capital of Mongolia. However, before getting there, we would have to cross through vast deserts. We had no idea if our plan was going to work. And we were always terrified of getting sent back to North Korea in case we failed.

❖

Suddenly, two shady-looking men approached us. They turned out to be the smugglers we'd been communicating with. We started heading toward their car, but once we were in the vehicle, we felt even less at ease. Instead of reassuring us and explaining to us what would happen, they immediately started asking us for the money. These two Chinese men, who were ethnically Korean, threatened us and demanded that we immediately take out our cash. My mother had a bad feeling about everything and took me outside in a frenzy.

"It's a trap!" Mom said to me. "All they want is to take our money from us! We can't leave our fate in the hands of these two thugs."

Distraught, we went to take refuge in a public sauna in this unfamiliar city. But had we really come all this way just to abandon our plans at the last minute? One of the two men called the cell phone we had saved up for before embarking on this journey and insisted that we complete the deal. Finally, we agreed to negotiate with them.

We made our way through a labyrinth of narrow, deserted streets and headed toward a small, dilapidated house on the outskirts of Erenhot. The two men led us into the first room. It was very dirty, and the only piece of furniture there was a bed. This house did not look like it was lived in very often; it looked more like a crack house. At the end of the room, there was a door that led to another room. There, we found three North Korean women. They were here for the same reason we were. But they had not spent even one yuan, because they were members of a Christian church that was paying for their trip to freedom. They were highly religious, which made us feel a little better, a little safer.

Later I would learn that American Protestant missionaries and South Koreans played a crucial role in getting North Korean escapees to Seoul. They have money, networks, and contacts in strategic places, and were willing to take big risks to help transpot North Koreans safely to South Korea. Their generosity was not without some self-interest, however. One of their objectives was to increase the number of followers in their community in Seoul. But this was hardly too much to ask, considering they were helping us escape from a life of tyranny and hiding.

Meeting these women made us feel a bit more at ease. After all, these smugglers knew what they were doing, right? With no better alternatives, we decided to take the risk. We took out our savings to pay the smugglers. The deal was done. We gave out twenty thousand yuan each to the two men. Had we just gotten swindled? We were about to find out.

❖

Our departure was scheduled for the second day, but we had to wait until night to make our escape, to minimize the risk of getting caught and subsequently repatriated to North Korea. The day seemed to drag on forever, especially since we had no say in our own departure plans. We were still unclear about what was going to happen to us, and how we were supposed to reach Seoul, which was far from here. The smugglers were, as always, taciturn.

Night finally started to descend over Erenhot, and then it was completely dark. Around ten p.m., the two men, still stoic, gave us the signal. It was time to go. In front of the house, an old, beat-up car was waiting for us. There were seven of us total, and we were supposed to fit in this piece of junk that was meant to hold at most five people. The two men took the front seats, and the five of us sat in the backseat, packed together like sardines. Since I was the smallest, I sat on the others' knees. The car jolted to a start and then crept along the deserted streets.

Then we reached the main streets, which were lit up by streetlamps. But after a quarter of an hour went by, they started to dim, until we were completely enveloped by darkness. There weren't any people or civilization around us for miles. Thanks to the white glow of the streetlamps there, I could see that the fields were starting to get more and more arid the farther we went. The trees, which were already sparse, gradually disappeared, and they were replaced with a scenery of rocks and the occasional shrub. We began to feel like we were in the middle of a desert.

After some time, we made our way off the asphalt road on to a bumpier path. Inside the car, you could cut the tension with a knife. The two men remained silent, and each one of us stayed lost in our thoughts, imagining the dangers in store during the next few hours. There was no going back now, but we still didn't know anything about our itinerary.

All of a sudden, in front of us, bright white lights lit up the night. Immediately, our driver turned off the headlights of the car and slowed down. As soon as he found a spot on the side of the road where he could do so, he pulled over and shut off the engine. The other car and its headlights were getting closer. The tension mounted higher and higher. We were desperately hoping that it wasn't the police or border patrols. The border patrols were a regular sight in this region. The vehicle continued approaching us without slowing down. It grew larger and larger before passing us, leaving a cloud of dust in its trail. Thankfully, it was just a regular car, not one containing uniformed men. The red lights on the back of the car started slowly disappearing. Outside, it was total darkness again, and we were enveloped by silence. Our driver turned the key, turned on the headlights, and soon we left our hiding spot to continue on the bumpy road.

That same situation happened only two more times during the hours that we were on the road. There weren't exactly a lot of people in the desert. Each time we saw lights in the distance, we held our breath. The driver, visibly tense, immediately hid on the side of the road, all lights turned off. Luckily, both times this happened, the car that rolled by contained neither police nor border guards, which meant we could continue on our mysterious journey through the night. We would continue along the Mongolian border until we found the safest passageway.

❖

After three hours on the road, our smugglers became more talkative. They explained in more detail what we were to expect. I understood that we were approaching a critical moment in our journey. I had butterflies in my stomach. For the first time, one of the two smugglers spoke to us in a gentle tone:

"Listen to me carefully. We are close to the border with Mongolia. When we arrive at the place that we know, you have to get out of the car and follow my instructions. Don't worry, we'll be right there beside you. We chose a very remote area where few people go. There will be a tall fence that you have to climb over. That's the Chinese border, guarded intermittently by patrolmen. We will help you climb it. When you land on the other side all you have left to do is go straight forward, as fast as possible. You will reach a second fence, which marks the entrance into Mongolian territory. Once you make it past the second barrier, you will be saved! The Chinese police will no longer have any power to arrest you. Understood?"

"And then? What will happen to us afterward?" asked one of our companions, very timidly.

The man replied, "Once you are on the other side, all you need to do is to give yourself up to the Mongolian army. They will transfer you to the South Korean embassy, in the capital city of Ulan Bator. There, the South Korean diplomats will take care of your transfer to Seoul. You will be safe there. Mongolia and South Korea have signed an agreement to send all North Korean escapees like you to South Korea. It will be fine!"

The smuggler was trying to reassure us right before we took off for a critical moment. The last thing he wanted was for us to start panicking when we were so close to the end. But his explanations, even if I appreciated them, didn't assuage my fears.

In the passenger side of the car, our anxiety was palpable. We knew that as soon as we crossed the first barrier, these men would take off with our money. We would have to manage by ourselves. And if we were arrested by the Chinese border police, then it was just too bad for us. They would have kept up their end of the bargain. And they would try this same operation again in a few weeks with other escapees. I still wasn't sure I completely trusted these men, who seemed motivated only by money. We couldn't afford to make any mistakes.

❖

After five hours, the driver slowed down and scrutinized the surrounding area and then turned off the ignition. It was three o'clock in the morning.

"Here we are," said the man.

He motioned for us to get out of the car, making sure we didn't make any noise.

It was really cold outside. It was May, but the night air was already very cool. In the darkness, I could distinguish some rocks and dirt, and then a tall, wooden stake. In front of us, there was a fence three meters tall. It was nicknamed the "green line" due to the color of the wooden stakes that ran along the border between Mongolia and China. The smugglers explained that they had chosen this spot because patrols were infrequent. But we still didn't have a minute to lose. The two men hoisted us up, one by one, over the barrier. The fence was quite tall, but I didn't have time to be scared. I was small and light and climbed the fence like a monkey, using the chain link like a ladder. My heart was racing. At the top of the fence, I paused for a moment to catch my breath and then climbed back down on the other side.

When my foot touched the ground, I didn't have any time to rejoice. I was too scared that a police officer would appear at any moment. I was even more scared because I sensed the nervousness of our smugglers on the other side of the fence. They didn't want to waste any time here, where they too were at risk for getting arrested. Since I was the youngest, I had to wait for my companions, who were heavier and less agile than I was and struggled a bit to climb the fence. Minutes passed, minutes that seemed to drag on forever. We had to hurry, because the most difficult part of our journey still remained: we had to reach the Mongolian border.

"Now run straight ahead! Get as far away as possible from China," whispered one of the smugglers. Shortly after, he disappeared through the darkness.

❖

And so began our mad run. The five of us bolted like we were being chased by an invisible monster. In front of me, the land seemed to move up and down as my feet sank into the sand. We ran and ran without looking back. We had to cross this no-man's-land as fast as possible to get to the Mongolian border, which was several miles away. As we weren't there yet, a Chinese policeman could bust us at any moment.

For an entire hour, we ran until we were out of breath. My mind was blank, concentrating only on reaching our destination. My breaths were short; we didn't speak to one another. My eyes started adjusting to the darkness, so I was able to distinguish the shapes—rocks and hills—in the distance. We were in the middle of the desert, an arid, desolate landscape that I'd never seen anywhere else before. Behind us, the sun seemed to already be rising. The time was passing by quickly and there was still nothing in sight. Could we be lost? I thought back to what the two men had told us:

"Go straight ahead!"

But how did we know whether we were going straight or not? There was no path to follow in this desert.

When we couldn't run anymore, we started walking. Finally, I was able to distinguish something through the dark. Something man-made. It was a sign placed on top of a cement base. On the side of the sign that we could see, there were sloppily painted Chinese characters that read *"Zhongguo,"* which means "China." On the other side there was something very messily written. I tried to decipher the gibberish and was able to make sense of only one word. I wasn't 100 percent sure, but I felt pretty confident that it said "Mongolia." What a relief! We were heading the right way. I caught my breath while waiting for the others. I was young, so I could walk fast, but for my mom and the others, it wasn't so easy.

I showed them what I'd found. But we weren't safe yet. As long as we hadn't crossed the Mongolian border, we were still at the mercy of the Chinese. And so we started running again, under a sky that was steadily growing brighter and brighter. How much longer would it take? Had the smugglers tricked us?

Finally, I stumbled upon what we were waiting for. In front of me was a fence, considerably shorter and in much worse condition than the one at the Chinese border. It matched the description that the smugglers had given us. We had no doubt; it was the Mongolian border! We had reached our goal. It was all the sweeter because this fence was not as tall as the Chinese one. Like spiders, we climbed as quickly as we could until we reached the top. After scaling the top, I clambered down the other side of the dilapidated fence.

I felt an immense relief. I relaxed for a moment and caught my breath. A massive weight had been lifted off my shoulders.

In a few minutes, the others made it over the fence as well. In that moment, we felt united by a strong sense of solidarity.

The other three women, who were highly religious, wanted to say grace to God. They took us by our hands and we formed a circle. The three of them praised Jesus out loud. For the first time in my life, I prayed. I felt overwhelmed by what we had gone through. Lost in the immensity of the desert, we were just a tiny, insignificant circle of people, but at least we had one another. Since I'm not religious, I stayed silent, but in my head I prayed that everything would go well.

During this time, daylight started to seep in around us, and I saw that our desert environs were quite majestic. It was five o'clock in the morning. The sun lit up the sand and the toffee-colored rocks. The horizon was empty, interspersed with rocky hills. The landscape was both marvelous and nerve-racking.

Later, in Seoul, while researching online, I would learn that we were in the Gobi Desert, one of the most arid deserts in the world. But at the time I didn't know that; I had no understanding of geography. Our sole objective was to march straight forth and surrender ourselves to the Mongolian army. It had been explained to us that they would transfer us to the South Korean embassy, because South Korea had signed an agreement with Mongolia to send defectors from North Korea to Seoul. We were about to find out if that was true.

❖

For the moment, our priority was simply to survive in the desert, since we had no provisions. The smugglers had given us each a bottle of water and a sausage link. Officially, the provisions were meager so that we wouldn't get weighed down during our trek, and because, according to them, we would quickly meet the hospitable Mongolians. But I was dubious. Where did we go now? Luckily, behind the fence, we stumbled upon a road. Finally, we would find civilization. All we had to do was follow it, and we'd surely find a village and people.

But after three hours of walking, we still hadn't seen a soul, and we started to feel doubtful, still traveling under the blisteringly hot sun. Were we on the right path? I was convinced that we were, but a few of the women weren't quite so sure and wanted to turn back. At that moment, my gut was telling me to keep going straight forward, so I told the others that I'd go ahead and scout things out.

In front of the group, I advanced through the gravel, and soon, through the blinding sunlight, I made out what looked to be a hut hidden in the desolate landscape. I was just about to go inform the others of my discovery, when all of a sudden, two uniformed men riding horses appeared. Seeing their horses, I no longer had any doubt: we were in Mongolia. I didn't know much about this country, but I knew that it had steppes and warriors on horses who had conquered China a long time ago, under the guidance of their leader Genghis Khan. Even the Chinese were afraid of these terrifying horsemen and bowed in their presence. In China, I had never seen border guards on horses. I was definitely in Mongolia. It was quite the sight. The men were almost as big as their horses. They galloped, whirled, and seemed resistant to the harsh climate of Mongolia, from the scorching summers to the harsh winters of negative thirty degrees Celsius (less than negative twenty Fahrenheit).

The two of them must have spotted me from afar. They quickly galloped over to our group. I was right: they were Mongolian soldiers. According to what I'd been told, they should not have been hostile. Yet the encounter did not go well. They searched all of us very roughly. They were clearly looking for money. Having found none, one of them started threatening us: "Give us all your cash, or else we'll send you straight back to the Chinese guards!"

I was quite worried, even if I wasn't sure I believed their blackmail. I had a sense they were taking their chances on us, seeing if they could pull the wool over our eyes. But they didn't look like they were ready to follow through. Especially since they had nothing to gain by taking us back to the Chinese border, which was several hours away. Besides, the smugglers had told us that there wasn't an agreement between China and Mongolia requiring Mongolia to send back North Koreans. What would the guards at the Chinese border do with five miserable North Koreans anyway?

They already had a hard enough time patrolling the "green line." They wouldn't want to worry about us; we would just be an extraneous burden. These soldiers were bluffing. I stood my ground, but it was our three companions who would get things under control, and in quite the unexpected way.

Our three comrades finally succeeded in cajoling these two horsemen thanks to their supplies...of cosmetics! Like good Koreans, they had brought tubes of creams and lotions, and they convinced these wretched soldiers with cracked and dirty hands of their beneficial effects on the skin. In Korea, skin quality is considered the first attribute of beauty for a woman. As soon as we had earned a bit of money in China, we had bought tubes and boxes of cosmetics to pamper ourselves and protect our skin. But we never would have thought to bring them with us across the desert. Our travel companions hadn't forgotten their makeup supplies, even for a perilous journey such as this one.

Satisfied with their new acquisitions, the officers locked us up temporarily in their barracks, where we waited the entire afternoon without knowing what was going to happen to us. And then, at night, a military vehicle tumbled in from the horizon, followed by a long trail of dust that floated up into the immense sky. This truck was obviously sent for us. Our Mongolian jailers were going to deliver us to the army.

The vehicle took us to a military base, which was also in the desert. There, the soldiers hid us away in a basement, in a building in the middle of nowhere, without giving us any explanation.

In this basement, I found women, children, and the elderly. Including us, there were a total of eighteen North Koreans who had tried to cross the desert in the last few days. We were no longer alone: we were part of an ever-growing group of refugees in search of liberty. It was reassuring to be part of such a group, even if we were still in captivity.

❖

For two weeks, we stayed there. The only things to eat were foul-smelling soup and fermented milk, which the Mongolians loved but that I quickly learned to hate. I had never missed *kimchi* so much before. No Korean can go for more than a few days without this spicy cabbage, fermented for several weeks in jars with red spices. Foreigners have a hard time getting used to this food that sets your mouth on fire and has a very strong taste. But for the Korean people, rice, meat, and vegetables are so bland without *kimchi*. It's as addictive as a drug, really. In the middle of that desert, I longed for my roots. And since I am a gastronome, I take deep pride in our national dish. I have survived through famines and situations that were much worse, but there, in that forsaken country where we didn't know what was to become of us, it was the lack of *kimchi* that would bother me the most.

❖

One day, when we no longer expected even the smallest of miracles to occur, the guards came to get us from our confinement area cave, and when we were released, we were shepherded into a military vehicle that transported us across the steppes of Mongolia toward the capital city, Ulan Bator. On the way there, we passed caravans of camels. It was the first time I'd seen these strange animals in real life. We were in the middle of nowhere, and no one knew if we would actually survive this long journey. Luckily, in this empty landscape, we started coming across more and more vehicles. I began to feel hopeful again, and it seemed to me that we were heading toward civilization—much better than being in the steppes. For just a few years in China, I had gotten a taste of city life, after our miserable life on the farm. I had truly become a city girl.

When we arrived in Ulan Bator, I couldn't believe my eyes: the sidewalks were cracked, the houses were dilapidated, and there was not a single skyscraper in sight. Everything was gray, dirty, and seemed to be in ruin. This run-down place could not be a capital city. After living in China, I was astonished at the sight of such a decrepit city.

However, it was in this broken, Soviet-style city that we were supposed to find our salvation.

But they did not let us go yet. We were sent into an enormous military base where seventy other North Koreans had been detained and were still waiting. How much longer was this going to take?

But at last, a pleasant surprise: we had rice and *kimchi*! The canteen was stocked by the South Korean embassy. We no longer felt abandoned; our brethren from the south seemed to be taking care of our departure. Furthermore, it was safer for us behind these high walls, since North Korea also has an embassy in Ulan Bator and could also "take care" of our departure. Outside the walls of the South Korean embassy, we risked falling into the hands of their agents. I didn't know if this fear had any basis in reality, but after all the trials and tribulations I had just gone through, I was prepared to expect anything.

❖

After three days of waiting, I was called in for an interrogation with a South Korean official. I was nervous, but Mom was right there next to me. I responded carefully to all the questions. They wanted to know everything: where I was from, how I'd gotten here, whether the woman next to me was really my mother. These questions were justified; South Korea was always on the lookout for possible spies from the north who would try to infiltrate the south. The two countries are still technically at war. The diplomats are also equally wary of Chinese citizens of Korean heritage who pretend to be defectors so that they can obtain visas for the economically well-off South Korea.

For a month, we were interrogated over and over again, each interviewer asking for more details than the last.

During this time, I got to know the other escapees quite well and realized that they had gone through many of the same things we had, but that my family and I had nonetheless been fairly lucky. We befriended a man who had become so dehydrated in the desert that he had had to drink his own urine. During his struggles with thirst and hunger, the two women who had been accompanying him disappeared in the vast sands of the desert.

I will never forget this man, whose health was rapidly deteriorating. He was in his fifties and had already tried several times to escape, but was sent back to North Korea, where he was savagely tortured. Weak-bodied and diabetic, he finally reached Mongolia, where he thought he would finally make it to freedom. But we had to watch him wither slowly, eaten away by his pain and suffering.

During one particularly sunny day, just a few steps away from me, he looked like he was having a seizure. He was shaking violently and frothing at the mouth. I was so scared. We immediately laid him down and called for help. But there was no medicine available here. Half an hour later, he was dead; he succumbed to the tribulations that he had had to endure up until now, which provoked this epileptic shock. Our group's morale just vanished. We begged the diplomats, in vain, to bury his body in Korea, our homeland. To this day, his body rests, alone, in Mongolia—so close to reaching the promised land of South Korea.

❖

After a month had passed, the interrogations finally stopped and we were all transferred to a camp on the outskirts of the city. At least it was summer, so we didn't have to suffer through the terrible Mongolian winter. We were much more comfortable in our new camp; there were only four of us in each room. Outside was the steppe, and we could go out and play soccer to kill the time.

There, we understood that we were on the last leg of our long journey, before boarding the airplane toward our new lives. The countdown had begun. Every week a vehicle came to take a group of defectors in the order that they had arrived.

However, our turn was behind schedule, because the departures were suspended for several weeks. And just like that we feared that there would be a problem at the last minute. But it was explained to us that the delay was simply because the South Korean president, Roh Moo-hyun, had just come to Mongolia on official business. I never quite understood exactly why that stopped us from leaving, but politics often don't make much sense to the politically disengaged. Perhaps the South Korean diplomats were simply too busy to worry about us?

After waiting two more months, it was finally our turn to leave via the Chinggis Khaan International Airport, about twelve miles from the city. I was already sick of Mongolia and its ever-changing weather, which was already cold even though it was only the end of summer. The smugglers who'd taken us to the Mongolian border had promised us that we'd be in Seoul within forty days, but it had already been four months.

❖

And our journey wasn't over yet. At the airport, with no explanation, we were put in a large gymnasium and had to wait yet another two weeks. Finally, one morning, the officials gave me a little green booklet with my photo, my name, and a stamp on one of its pages. At the time, I had no idea this was a passport. It was only later that I learned the significance of what I was given that day.

Then they brought us to the airport and loaded us onto a big airplane. They recommended that we not talk to anyone during the flight.

When the engines started whirring, I sat back in my seat.

I had never flown on an airplane before, but after all I'd gone through, I thought that it couldn't be so bad. And when the plane took off, I watched through the window as the airport become smaller and smaller until it disappeared.

It was only at that moment that I finally felt that we were saved. I was overcome with a vast sense of relief. While we were in Mongolia, I constantly feared that something bad was going to happen to us. But now, on this plane, we were en route toward South Korea, under the care of the South Korean authorities. No one could stop us now. It seemed unbelievable, but we had finally made it.

The plane was not completely full, and everything went smoothly during our three-hour flight. We were even served lunch. We were just a small group of North Korean defectors among the rest of the passengers, who probably had no idea who we were, nor what we had experienced before arriving at this point.

The plane started making its descent and my ears started hurting. The captain announced that we would soon arrive in Incheon, South Korea's international airport. I looked out the window and saw the sea, and the magnificent beaches that cut through the blue water. It was September, and the sun was shining brightly. *I've made it to heaven*, I thought.

❊ 15

The plane vibrated as it touched ground. The engine roared as the plane braked to a stop. A million thoughts were dashing around in my head. In a scratchy voice over the loudspeakers, the captain welcomed us to South Korea.

Since then, dozens of defectors have told me about the immense joy they felt at this exact moment, when the plane reached South Korean ground. But for me, as the plane rolled along the runway, I held confused and conflicting emotions inside. On the one hand, I felt relieved. After years of suffering and hardships, I knew that at last, the Chinese police would never again be able to send us back to a North Korean jail. But on the other hand, I was also very worried. We had no idea what was in store for us in this strange and

foreign land. How were we going to survive in this new country, where we had not a single friend or family member?

When the airplane came to a halt, the passengers stood
up to file out the front door. Our small group, however,
stayed seated, as we had been instructed to do. Once the
airplane was empty, we were let out the back. A bus was
waiting for us on the runway. As we got onto the bus and
the doors closed behind us, the bus started up and crossed
the seemingly never-ending runway, before passing through
a gate and reaching another highway. Here I was in South
Korea, and I hadn't even seen the inside of the airport.

❖

Through the window, with my eyes wide open, I gazed upon
my new country. I was amazed by how clean it looked. As
we drove along, we saw more and more high-rise apartments,
and there were more and more streets. It didn't immediately register that we were in Seoul. In China, I had gotten
used to large cities like Shanghai. My first culture shock
upon seeing an urban area was when we arrived in Dalian,
directly from the countryside. I had been startled to see
such wide streets and the intrepid pedestrians next to us,
who contrasted sharply with the malnourished people from
the countryside. I remember especially clearly our first time
in a shopping mall. In just one hour, I saw more commer-
cial goods than I had ever seen before in my life. We had

spent the afternoon marveling at every store. A few hours later, we had walked out of the enormous market with nothing but a simple bottle of water in our hands. It was all we could afford. In Dalian, our shopping cart was almost always empty, and my mom told me that it was her dream to one day be able to afford to fill it up.

❖

Here in South Korea, our bus stopped in front of a building surrounded by a concrete wall with barbed wire at the top. We all filed off. A man in uniform frisked us, checked our documents, and conducted a quick interrogation. Then each of us received a package of clothing, a toothbrush, and toothpaste. I wound up in a room with five other women. Compared to the room where I'd lived in Mongolia, everything was so comfortable, clean, and warm. I felt reassured. I stayed here six days while waiting for my oral interrogation. It was the last test, the test that was to decide my future. If I passed, then I would be eligible for South Korean citizenship. I felt confident, but I knew that I still needed to remain calm and focused.

❖

Then the day arrived. When it was my turn, the guards separated me from my mother and threw me into a cell. I was to be cut off from all communication with the rest of the world during the investigation. The tiny window in the room allowed for only a small ray of sunshine and a glimpse of the streets outside. To alleviate my boredom, I pressed my face against the glass and stared at the passersby, dreaming of becoming free like they were, on the outside. I felt like a prisoner in here. To pass time, I slept a lot.

And then the daily interrogations commenced, and continued seemingly without end. They were led by the Korean National Intelligence Service (NIS). Their aim? To identify any North Korean spies who were trying to infiltrate South Korea, as the two sides of the peninsula were still officially at war.

Each day, I had to retell my story, recounting every detail of my life in Eundeok and our escape. I had to give dates, addresses, and names that I no longer remembered. I had to do this every single day. Sometimes, I mixed some of the details up. The interrogator was polite, but pushed me.

"You say this, but your mother gave us a different version."

Mom was being interrogated at the same time, but I wasn't allowed to see her.

"Is she really your biological mother?"

I held my breath.

"Did you offer sexual services while you were in China, like your peer X did?"

At this point, I had a lump in my throat and couldn't bring myself to speak.

Before we were separated, my mom and I had agreed to leave out the detail about my little brother. It was something she felt very embarrassed about. But after two days, my interrogator took me by surprise, telling me that he knew all about my little brother. Mom must have cracked under the pressure. Trapped, I admitted everything as well.

In hindsight, I realize that this little detail had no ill effect on our file. Our situation would have been a bit more risky if we had been members of the Workers' Party back in North Korea. In that case, the interrogators would have suspected that we were spies sent by the north to collect intelligence about South Korea.

❧

There was something else on my mind that kept me awake at night: Keumsun, who was still in Shanghai. Since we left China, we had not been able to communicate with her at all. We'd told her that we'd be in Seoul in forty days, like the smugglers had promised us, and that we would call her cell phone as soon as we arrived. However it had already been more than four months, and we had not been able to call her. We tried once in Mongolia, but to no avail. She must have been worried to death. And so, starting at my first interrogation, I begged the men on the other side of the table to let me make a call to China, just once. But these NIS workers were uncompromising and told me I was not permitted to contact anyone during my interrogation. I was desperate, so I insisted over and over that they let me call my sister just once, to let her know that we were still alive. Alas, for a long time, all my efforts were in vain.

Finally, seeing how desperate I was, they decided to do me a favor. I was allowed to make a call lasting three minutes, and not one second longer.

Grabbing the receiver, I dialed Keumsun's number. I shook with neves as the phone rang. I held my breath. The phone's sound was of poor quality, but even then, I recognized Keumsun's voice immediately.

"Big sister, is that you? It's Eunsun! We're alive; I'm in Seoul with Mom."

When Keumsun responded, I broke out in tears at the sound of her voice. I cried tears of joy while gripping the receiver tightly. As usual, Keumsun was the stronger one. At the other end of the line, she kept her calm. But with the officers keeping track of the time, I had not a second to lose. I quickly gave her all the essential information.

"I can't talk for long, because I'm being interrogated right now, but don't worry, everything's going fine. Mom's doing well too. As soon as we can get out of here, we'll call you to tell you everything."

When I hung up, I felt a massive sense of relief. I went back to face my interrogators. I was still locked in a cell, but nothing could bother me anymore. I had just relieved myself of an immense burden.

The questioning started once more, again with no end in sight. Overall, my interrogations went fairly smoothly, especially since I later learned that some people were forced to take lie detector tests.

After a week of discussion, everything stopped for three days. It was the holidays in this country. I walked in circles in my room. After the three days were up, things resumed exactly as they'd been going. It all seemed so . . . fastidious, interminable, exaggerated to me. Would we have risked our lives as we'd done and gone through such hardships if we were spies? My pride was a little wounded. I didn't appreciate them questioning my honest intentions.

❖

One day, however, the torment ended, and I was allowed to return to the living quarters and see my mom. Finally, we could speak to each other. I began to understand that I had passed the final test. Our morale improved dramatically. All the more so because we were finally allowed outside for some fresh air. We were treated to a picnic at the top of the tallest building in Korea, the 63 Building. It was a tall tower of salmon-colored glass that glistened under the sunlight. At such a height, the view was phenomenal, with the river below our feet and the mountains in the horizon. We could never quite forget that we were still in police custody, however. They also drove us to a shopping center to buy some new clothes. They paid for us, but they had no fashion sense. But we didn't mind, we would take whatever they gave us. We were finally being taken care of, fed, clothed—it would have been quite churlish for us to complain.

After a month, we were told that we were being transferred to a special center to learn how life worked in South Korea. All defectors from the north had to pass through this center, called Hanawon, where we took an accelerated ten-week course on capitalism. However, this course seemed to me just as painful as the interrogations. Once more, I found myself locked inside with a bunch of poorly educated, coarse people. There were disagreements all the time in the rooms. During the day, we would take theoretical courses where we were taught about the history of Korea, the capitalist system, and how South Korean society functioned. It was abstract and very boring. From time to time, we would be allowed to leave the premises for a "practical experience." A visit to the post office, for example, where we were shown how to send a package. Then we were brought to a bank where we were taught how to use an ATM. I was both fascinated and completely lost. I didn't understand any of the explanations; I come from an entirely different world, and I had no concept of the financial systems that were being explained to me.

In order to make up for my many years off from education, I decided to take classes with teenagers, instead of with adults, every Wednesday and Thursday. For the first time since we left Eundeok, I returned to school. It was a shock for me. I started learning about math, literature, and history again, after a hiatus of nine years. And I started to learn a little bit of English.

At Hanawon, I typed Korean for the first time on a computer. In China, I had been to an Internet café once or twice, but since I didn't really know much about computers or IT, it didn't do much for me. Here, I was taught about technology. I was also surprised to learn that South Korea was one of the most technologically advanced countries in the world. But this reintegration into my studies was hard. I didn't remember having to put so much effort into schoolwork before. I had forgotten everything. And I, the former good student of Eundeok, started to doubt my abilities in the presence of these youths who were much quicker to learn than I was.

Fortunately, the time went by quickly, and the day we were allowed to leave Hanawon finally arrived. One day, we were told that we would be taking photos for our ID cards. I was so excited. It was a momentous occasion. I finally felt that I was really going to become a citizen. That morning, my mom and I tried to make ourselves look pretty using what means we had. I found a little bit of makeup, and did my best. This photo was so important to me. A childhood memory surfaced, of when Papa and I had taken that photo in the little photo shop in Eundeok. It seemed so long ago, from another lifetime.

When the camera flashed, I put all my efforts into looking my best. But when I saw the result, I was disappointed. I did not look as nice as I had hoped. Naïvely, I told myself that they were probably going to touch up the photo a little. I quickly learned, however, that they had more important things to worry about. But this photo, even if I didn't like it, was an important milestone for me. It meant that we were going to have official papers soon. Above all, it meant that we would soon be free, outside, living like real South Koreans. At least, that's what I hoped. Every week, a group consisting of seven or eight defectors left Hanawon to enter the outside world. We started counting the days until we could leave. The time had almost come.

❖

After nearly three months of classes that were often quite dull, the day finally came. I will remember this date forever: December 28, 2006. The night beforehand, we packed all our belongings in cardboard boxes. The morning of the

twenty-eighth, we got on the bus and said good-bye—
forever—to our life as fugitives.

Accompanied by seven other defectors, we rode in silence to Seoul and to our new lives. On the way there, we
had to make a stop to take care of a few last administrative tasks before continuing our lives in South Korea. First,
we stopped by the administrative center of the district where
we were going to live from now on. There, I received my
South Korean ID. For the first time in nine years, I no longer
had to live in hiding! It was such a burden lifted off my shoulders. Even if, in the moment, I didn't quite realize everything it represented.

Finally, we were brought to a bank to open an account.
In Hanawon, we had learned to our great delight that the
government financially supports defectors to help them
settle down in South Korea. It was such a wonderful surprise
to discover this country's hospitality. After fighting, with
my best efforts, to survive in misery since I was eleven, this
financial aid package was something I wasn't expecting.
More than ever, I was sure that it had been a good idea for
us to come to South Korea, to leave behind our illegal status in Shanghai.

I received eight million won (at the time, about the equiv-
alent of six thousand five hundred dollars) and my mom
received twenty million (just a bit over sixteen thousand
dollars). But the rent in Seoul was so high that fifteen million

were immediately put to use to cover the costs of our apartment. When we got to the bank, our money had already
been transferred to the owner of the apartment.

We were given the terms of our bank accounts, and the
numbers of our bank cards. We were ready. We were now
"normal" South Koreans. The only thing left for us to do
was to explore our new apartment.

❖

Night was falling when the bus dropped us off in front of
our final destination. I got off, leaving behind me forever
those three transitional months that had felt so much longer. Finally, we could start our new life. But for the moment,
I was exhausted after such a long day.

In front of us, there was an immense apartment complex. There were thousands of these in South Korea. This
building had fifteen floors. It appeared a bit worn out and
was at least twenty years old. I wasn't expecting anything
amazing, but still, I was a bit surprised. However after a
year of wandering, it was luxury. After so many years, for
the first time since leaving Eundeok, I would have a place
to call my own. My joy was indescribable. With my mom,
I headed toward the building in this unfamiliar city that
would become our home.

According to the instructions given to us during the bus
ride, the final step was to go to the office that managed the

building. There, someone would be waiting for us to hand over the keys to the apartment.

Timidly, we walked into the room on the first floor. A woman was indeed waiting for us. She coldly received us, checked our names, and completed her tasks without offering us the least word of welcome.

"I already cleaned the place for you. Here are your keys, you are in building 805, apartment 804. It's on the ninth floor. To get there, you have to cross the main courtyard."

And then she sent us on our way. Each of us with a little bag, we walked across the courtyard to building 805.

We took the elevator up to the ninth floor. When we arrived at our apartment, I put the key in the keyhole and turned, and the door opened. I walked in and turned on the lights. In accordance with Korean tradition, we took off our shoes when we walked in, and headed toward the kitchen. To the left, a door led to a small room. It was the living room. On the floor, there was a set of large footprints consisting of dried mud. To the left, we found another little room, which even had a veranda. There were three rooms for us in this place, a veritable palace compared to what we had been living in.

The apartment was empty and dirty. There was no furniture anywhere and the gas didn't work. The place was covered with dust. The people who lived there last had left it in a deplorable state. The woman we'd met downstairs had told us she had cleaned the place, but she was obviously lying.

And so, to help us really feel at home, we started to clean the place, using what we had. At that point in our lives, we couldn't tell whether we were living in reality or simply dreaming.

After an hour of cleaning, we opened up the four cardboard boxes in the living room. They had been delivered sometime during the day, before we got there. These boxes contained all the possessions we had in the world, given to us at the Hanawon center. Clothes, blankets, a rice cooker ... they were secondhand items donated to us by charity, specifically, by churchgoers, we were told. It was so heartening to see other people willing to help us settle into our new lives.

Outside, night was falling over Seoul. The city lights lit up the night sky with an intensity that couldn't be found in North Korea. This metropolis really seemed to have no limits.

Mom and I explored every nook and cranny of the apartment. In this empty apartment, we suddenly felt a little lonely. For the first time since leaving Eundeok, we were truly alone in the world, just the two of us, with even Keumsun absent. There had been no one here waiting for us, and we didn't know anyone in this building, this city,

or even this country, which from this day forth was to be
our home.

❖

It seems absurd and ungrateful, but all of a sudden, after
making it all the way to South Korea and obtaining the papers that we never imagined we'd receive, after the sheer
joy of this day when we had finally and totally escaped from
our life of hiding, after being welcomed and housed in this
new country, I was overcome by an immense feeling of sadness. It was as if everything, all the burdens and hardships
of the past nine years, came back to me at that moment.
The future loomed ahead like unfamiliar territory we had
to conquer. I was overwhelmed. Mom must have been feeling the same way.

After cleaning the place a little more thoroughly, we gave
in to our fatigue and fell asleep. We didn't have dinner, since
we didn't have any food in the apartment, and we had neither the courage nor the desire to venture down into the
city to buy something.

And so I took out and unfolded our four blankets and
laid them out side by side in the center of the room. Mom
and I lay down over them. I snuggled up against her. We
turned off the lights. Warmed by each other's body heat,
we fell asleep.

❋ 16

As soon as we settled down a little, we got to work right away at building our new lives. As always, our priority was to find a way to support ourselves. The financial aid offered by the government was only enough to last us a few months in this country, where the cost of living was even higher than in China, never mind North Korea.

We had it all planned out. Mom was going to find a job while I went back to school. I would finally be able to make up my nine years without schooling, before it was too late to ever return to school. We were not about to rest on our laurels and play the role of tourists in South Korea.

Soon, my mom found a full-time job as a babysitter. It was a common profession in this country, because there were very few day-care centers, and mothers who wished to continue their careers had to rely on nannies to take care of their children. And so, my mom left to go stay with a family that lived far away from us. She only came home once every fifteen days.

For one year, I essentially lived alone in that big apartment. I was enrolled in school, and schoolwork occupied most of my days, since in South Korea you had to study well into the night if you wanted to stay afloat among your classmates.

Living alone was a new challenge that helped develop my character. I learned to take care of issues that arose in day-to-day life, and to find a balance in the way I spent my time. I had quite a hard time at first. Since I had almost no free time, I rarely did any cooking and ate out most of the time, like a lot of other South Koreans. There are so many cheap and enticing restaurants here. In the mornings, I usually didn't eat breakfast, and instead drank a glass of milk. In fact, for the first few weeks, I would drink several glasses a day ... until I started having stomachaches, which I soon learned were caused by my overconsumption of milk. I'd never drunk so much milk in my life. How ironic: I, someone who survived through a famine, was now suffering from overconsumption!

After the initial agony and solitude, I quickly started to make friends at school. I was five years older than my classmates. At first, I didn't tell anyone about my age or background, for fear of being seen in a negative light. But then, little by little, I started answering others' questions and telling my story. It was so empowering to be able to live in freedom here in Seoul. Life here was hectic, fun, and sometimes also very hard, but it was never boring. There were so many attractions to be seen. After school, my new friends from class would take me to grab a quick bite to eat, usually *tteokbokki*, these little rice cakes soaked in a spicy red sauce that were the favorite snack of students. Then we would all go sing karaoke together. In this society which, to me, sometimes seems self-centered, I needed this group of friends, this feeling of solidarity that I had had while in North Korea and that I had been missing so dearly since coming here.

❖

Over time, I started to feel more and more at ease here. Maybe it was because I was young, so it was easier for me to adapt to a new environment than it was for my mother's generation. Soon enough, I start to extol the merits of life in South Korea to my sister, who was still in Shanghai. It was my dream for her to join us. We started talking regularly via telephone, telling each other about our lives. Keumsun was happy in China, but it wasn't really because of the country. It was because she was still in love, and her boy-friend, a Chinese soldier, treated her so well.

Sometime in mid-2007, she told me a secret:

"I'm pregnant, but don't tell Mom yet."

I held my tongue, but months passed by, and eventually she had to share the news with Mom as well. She was expecting a baby girl. At the end of 2007, she married her Chinese boyfriend, so that she could "officialize" her situation. The marriage was just administrative; there was no reception or ceremony. But she was getting by just fine in Shanghai. Using fake identification papers, she had managed to officially marry a soldier in the People's Liberation Army! She was able to achieve this through the cunning of her father-in-law, who absolutely adored her. The fake papers that she used originally were good enough to land her a small job, but not to get married. So her father-in-law did something rather ingenious: he bought the papers of a young lady who had passed away recently. Everything was possible in China if you had the money . . . and voilà, Keumsun married under a false name, but using real identification. I was blown away by his ingenuity.

Keumsun was lucky to have found such generous in-laws. Her parents-in-law loved her and treated her like she was a princess, and they spoiled their new granddaughter. Keumsun happily went to stay with them near Hangzhou, not far from Shanghai, while her husband was away in the barracks. She didn't have to cook or do chores, she told me over the phone. Such a situation was quite rare.

After learning all of this about her life in China, I realized how difficult it would be to persuade her to come join us in Seoul.

❖

In January 2008, we had been in South Korea for just over a year. Mom had saved some money on the side, and it was currently my winter break. Thus, it was set: we would go to China to visit my older sister and celebrate the birth of her daughter. It was possible because now we were true South Koreans, and no longer illegal migrants. We no longer had anything to risk by going to China. Secretly, we had another motivation for this trip, too: we went with the intention of persuading Keumsun to come back with us to Seoul.

We took the plane for Shanghai, and then on to Hangzhou. It was truly wonderful to see each other again. But Keumsun had no desire to go to South Korea, as she was doing so well with her new family. Besides, she had a charming baby girl to take care of. So, sadly, we returned to Seoul without her.

However, over time, through phone call after phone call, we convinced her to reconsider. I missed her so much that I used any argument I could think of to try to persuade her to join us.

"One day, your cover-up might be discovered, and if you get caught there will be big consequences. It would be in

your best interest to come here and become a South Korean citizen, make some money, and then you can go back
to China without incurring any danger."

It was indeed true that South Korea was more developed
than China and that, if you were willing to work hard, you
could earn a lot more money here.

A few weeks later, Keumsun was convinced. She agreed
to come join us, at least temporarily. I was so happy to hear
her say that!

But there was still the issue of how she was going to leave
China and travel here. She had a "real" Chinese ID, but not
a passport, which was required to leave the country. And
if she applied for one, the authorities would almost definitely
figure out that the ID she was using didn't belong to her.
The only solution was for her to leave illegally through another country, just as we had done.

❖

I quickly found the phone number of the smugglers who'd
helped us in 2006. They didn't seem particularly enthusiastic, but we had now learned to trust and respect them,
because they'd kept their word to us.

To assuage Keumsun's qualms, we promised her VIP
treatment. She would be able to leave China without having to walk through the Mongolian desert. Since arriving
in Seoul, we had learned that it was easy to organize the

transport of a North Korean to South Korea without traveling through any deserts. The smugglers could provide a fake South Korean passport to permit the person fleeing to board an airplane to South Korea. Upon landing at Incheon Airport, all the North Korean escapee has to do was turn him or herself in to the authorities, and everything would be taken care of from there. There was no need to risk your life on the "green line" fences or in the Gobi Desert. Everything was possible ... as long as you were able to pay.

The smugglers asked for ten million won (about ten thousand dollars), around three times more than what our passage through Mongolia had cost me and my mom. Mom asked for a discount for her daughter, reminding them that we were "loyal customers." She negotiated with them until finally we got a nice discount: we would only have to pay seven and a half million won.

❖

In May 2008, with a fake passport in hand, Keumsun left China for South Korea. She left behind her husband, at least for the time being, as well as her young daughter, whom she asked her in-laws to care for. Again, her family members and her husband showed themselves to be quite noble and generous. They understood her decision and they trusted her. They knew that she was going to return one day, as soon as she had made some money and acquired a real South

Korean passport. I really appreciated their family and thought that Keumsun was quite lucky for having married into it.

But at the last minute, Keumsun's trip was put on hold. The smuggler had promised her an airplane ticket, but at the eleventh hour, for whatever strange reason, her itinerary was changed. Finally, she was able to hop on a boat and cross the Yellow Sea, and she ended up on South Korean territory. Following the instructions given to her, she turned herself in to customs as a North Korean defector.

She was taken in and interrogated by the NIS, just like we were. After a month, she was released—the interrogations had gone well. And when she got out, she managed to avoid the three months in Hanawon that we'd been subjected to. At the time, the center was overwhelmed by the number of defectors. In 2008, more than 2,800 North Koreans arrived in South Korea after long and perilous journeys like the one we went through. Hanawon was at capacity, and since Keumsun already had family in the country, she was allowed to skip the training there.

❖

And so she came to stay with us. It felt so good to be together again! As usual, Keumsun adapted fast, all the while maintaining her independence. However, her heart was still in China, with her husband and her family. She still contacted them on a regular basis. Every day, she spoke to her husband on the computer. The two of them were inseparable. Her husband seemed to be very much in love with her. Sometimes, Keumsun told him she was too busy to talk for long. She hid her grief very well, but under her calm appearance, I knew that she longed to be with her husband and family. One day, I found an empty bottle of *soju*, a Korean liquor. Keumsun must have been drinking away her sorrows. But she was too discreet to talk about it.

Fortunately, twice a year, for a month at a time, Keumsun was able to see her family in China, who welcomed her with open arms. When her husband finished his military service, she would return to the country of her parents-in-law. She and her husband were excited to be able to raise their daughter together.

It was during this time that I mapped out my future in Seoul. At the age of twenty-two, I made the decision to attend college after I finished with my remedial classes, instead of constantly working small jobs to earn money. I was hesitant, because my studies sometimes felt tedious, difficult, and unrewarding. In China, I had learned to get by on my own, to take charge of my own life, to learn on the job the way adults do. And in Seoul, I found myself in school again, the oldest in the class, with classmates less mature than

I was but often much better educated. It was humbling to see how much more the younger students knew than I did, so I had to work very hard to catch up.

Finally, I decided for sure to go to college. I realized that if I wanted to get a good job in South Korea, tertiary education was necessary. The job market was so competitive here, and education was of paramount importance.

The only issue was that this was no easy task. In South Korea, a lot of parents start preparing their children for entrance into the nation's best universities from kindergarten. They often hire English teachers to start tutoring their sons and daughters from a very young age. Additionally, during their adolescent years, the students go to after-class study schools known as *hagwon* late into the night. I, on the other hand, having been out of school for nine years, was at a serious disadvantage.

Fortunately, Sogang University, a Catholic school and one of the most prestigious in the country, offers a special program for students from North Korea like me. Unlike South Korean students, we didn't have to take an exam to be accepted to the school. Instead, we just needed to have an interview. And our tuition fees were also waived. It was an incredible opportunity and I decided to take it. There were about forty of us North Koreans at Sogang University. Without this kind of program, it would be nearly impossible for students like us to have a good career in this country.

I want to take the chance here to thank those who created this program and provided me with such an opportunity.

My admissions interview for Sogang University went well, and I decided on a major in Chinese Literature and Civilization. I had to use my strengths to make up for the weaknesses in my education, and because I spent many years in China, I had a head start in Chinese studies. I got lucky, because in other subjects, I wasn't quite as strong. Still, I always tried my best.

My family—the family that was currently working so hard in a South Korean supermarket to help support my education—had high hopes for me. Mom and Keumsun had found jobs in the cafeteria of the supermarket Homeplus, which wasn't far from the apartment where we were living together. They slept in the living room and let me use the only bedroom so that I could study during late hours and get some rest during the night.

Often when I woke up in the morning, I felt like staying in bed rather than going to class, as a result of staying up too late studying. Luckily, my professors helped me make up my lost years and kept encouraging me to continue. Particularly my English professor, Noh Jae-hoon, who came to school very early in the morning, before classes started, to give me makeup lessons and always encouraged me.

❖

A lot of South Koreans have been very helpful to me these last few years, and I want to thank them from the bottom of my heart.

Others are indifferent, and some maintain their distance from me. They are wary of those from the north—the "enemies." Don't forget that officially, the two Koreas are still technically at war, and have been since 1950. Some South Koreans don't like that we, the defectors, benefit from the system, thanks to government aid. And yet, I have a South Korean passport and I have the right to vote. I am just as much a citizen as everyone else here. But some people, both young and old, don't think of me as an equal. They treat me like they treat immigrants from Southeast Asia, the Philippines, or Cambodia; the "poor people" they despise so much.

Sometimes, during my conversations with other students at the university, people would tell me that they opposed the reunification of the two Koreas, because they didn't want their tax money to go toward paying for the "poor" North Koreans. I was sometimes hurt at hearing people say things like this. What the newspapers said also shocked me, because they often talked about the totalitarian regime founded by Kim Il-sung and the North Korean population as one and the same, even though North Koreans are the regime's primary victims. South Korea hasn't always been the promised land of Eden, but it has welcomed us and we are thankful for the opportunity to live here.

In those early years in South Korea, whenever we felt sad or lonely, my mom, Keumsun, and I would sit in a circle in the apartment during the evening and turn off the lights. In the darkness, we would tell stories about the past and sing North Korean songs until the end of the night. But rest assured, we were not apologists for Kim Jong-il's regime. It is just that sometimes we miss our homeland, and sometimes we're prone to nostalgia. We are not ungrateful, but I think it is normal to sometimes reminisce about the happier memories of childhood.

❖

I had a lot of North Korean friends who were escapees like me. Among them was my boyfriend, who had escaped from one of the Kim regime's notorious labor camps. When I met him, he was a journalism intern in Seoul at the *Dong-A Ilbo*, one of the big daily newspapers in the country. He came to interview me for an article he was writing about North Korean refugees who were students in South Korea. And so began a story of how two North Koreans fell in love on the other side of the "iron curtain."

My boyfriend hated North Korea's Stalinist regime with a passion. With him by my side, I started to develop my own political views, and I realized the extent of the horrors committed by the dictatorship. In his opinion, I wasn't critical enough of the regime. He was very politically minded and wanted to see the regime collapse, while the majority of defectors in South Korea maintain a low profile and prefer to focus their efforts on integrating themselves into South Korean society. I understood my boyfriend's passion, but for me, my motivation was a little different. More so than toppling the dictatorship, I wanted to give a voice to my people to the north who had been forgotten by the world.

To keep my spirits up, I started to participate in a hiking club for North Koreans. Certain weekends, we would climb the tall mountains that surround Seoul. We helped one another and also had a lot of fun doing so. I also started attending a Protestant church led by a North Korean pastor. I was not particularly religious, but at least now I felt like I was part of one big family.

Sometimes, the family element seems to be missing in this country, whose economy is so vibrant, but where everyone follows his or her own path without always paying attention to the people around them. This feeling is made all the stronger because, even though I consider myself to have successfully integrated into South Korean society, there are still things that distinguish me from other South Koreans and make me feel closer with my fellow compatriots from the north. Immigrants always seem to have this kind of nostalgia, though it doesn't diminish our gratitude toward our new country.

✿

Today, while I write this, I am twenty-five years old, and I have plans for the future. Here, I can dream of doing things that I didn't even know existed during my former life. I have been able to start learning about the world. I even went to Russia last year! I traveled to Siberia thanks to a prize that I won along with my friends from the debate team, a club I participated in. We came first place in a competition, and the first-place prize was a trip to Siberia for a week.

I was excited to fly on an airplane again. It was the first time that I had ever traveled for leisure in my life. And besides, we were so proud of ourselves for winning the competition. How could I have even thought this would be possible just a few years ago, living in the misery that was Chongjin?

In Russia, my classmates and I came across quite the surprise. One day, while we were in downtown Vladivostok, we came across some workers on a construction site. Our guide told us that they were North Koreans sent by the Kim Jong-il regime to work overseas and bring foreign currency back to the country. My eyes lit up with curiosity. The guide explained to us that when the men were sent here to work, the regime made their wives and children stay behind as collateral, to make sure that these workers wouldn't escape, like we had, from the "socialist paradise" founded by Kim Il-sung.

Upon seeing these workers, I felt my heart break. I naturally felt drawn toward them. I was burning with the desire to speak to them. But that would, without a doubt, only bring trouble to all of us. And what if there were North Korean police officers around? The images of our interrogations at the border, after we were arrested in China, ran through my head. It would be a terrible risk. Sadly, I left these poor compatriots of mine without speaking to them.

❖

In Seoul, I have built a new life for myself. I feel at ease here. My favorite place to spend time is a little café near my apartment called Doctor Robin. I often spend hours there with my white laptop studying or just daydreaming. There, I feel at ease. I like calm environments and dislike loud noise.

Life in South Korea has presented me with another gift: here, I feel that if I believe in something, I can accomplish it. It is a hope without any cost. My first objective is to get my college diploma, and then to get a master's degree, though I'm not sure in what subject yet. But before that, I'm going to take a gap year to reflect, improve my English, and perhaps travel and discover the world. I'm also trying to earn a scholarship to study in America. It would be an incredible opportunity, so my fingers are crossed.

Later down the line, I want a career where I can give hope to others. I imagine myself becoming a child psychologist. When I was in China, I saw so many children without mothers, I saw so many boys and girls abandoned and left to fend for themselves, that I began to realize the importance of childhood in the construction of a personality. Maybe it is because my childhood was in part stolen from me. Maybe it is also because I still think about my brother, whose fate worries me to no end.

The summer he was eleven years old, the three of us—my mom, Keumsun, and I—went back to China to see him during our vacation. As I said earlier, with our South Korean passports, we had nothing left to fear.

We arranged this trip via telephone with my brother's father, the farmer, and we planned to meet at Yangzi, a city in the north of China where there is a strong Korean community. We promised to take the farmer and my brother around China on a tourism trip, and to pay for everything ourselves.

After a night on a boat on the Yellow Sea and a long train ride, we walked up to the spot where we had arranged to meet up, in front of an enormous shopping mall. My heart was beating so fast I thought it was going to jump out of my chest. I was going to see my little brother again! He was two years old when I left him. Would he still recognize me? There was also some apprehension in the air, particularly for my mom. For the first time since we'd left for Shanghai, we were going to see the farmer, the man who had made us suffer so much.

On the sidewalk of downtown Yangzi, the crowd swarmed around us, and I wondered if I was going to recognize them. They had probably changed quite a bit. But in fact, we had no difficulty finding them. Standing in front of the entrance, the man and the little boy were easy to distinguish: in the middle of these businessmen, they looked like hobos, with their dirty and tattered clothes. I felt sorry for them, and I was quickly overcome with pity. Our eyes met, and we recognized each other immediately and made our way through the crowd. Our reunion went well. The farmer smiled and seemed genuinely happy to see us—it was quite surprising. He had aged a bit; his hair had grayed and his skin was more sunburned than ever before.

My little brother hardly paid any attention to me and behaved like a coarse and uncouth preadolescent. I quickly became shocked by his lack of manners and lack of education. At the restaurant, he behaved like a spoiled, poorly raised child, and acted on his every whim. I tried to talk to him, but the only thing he was interested in was playing with my iPhone. Right away, I decided to go buy him some new clothes, so that he would look presentable. Mom had been sending a hundred thousand won (about a hundred dollars) to the farmer each month to help her son. It was not considered a large sum in South Korea, but in the Chinese countryside, it was not a negligible amount. Alas, it looked like the farmer was keeping the money for himself, rather than spending it on his son. Sometimes, we also sent clothes to my brother. When we asked the farmer what he'd done with the clothes, he nonchalantly responded that he'd sold them all. I felt so disheartened.

Then we took our trip to Shanghai as tourists. We wanted to make the farmer and my brother happy, but the longer we spent together, the angrier I felt. My mother was financing the entire voyage using the money that we had worked so hard to earn, while my little brother and his peasant father behaved like dirty freeloaders. We went to an amusement park in Shanghai, and we even saw a 3-D movie—the tickets cost a fortune!—and yet my little brother always asked for more. And his father didn't say anything about it.

I told myself that we couldn't let this child remain in such conditions, at the hands of this barbaric farmer. I wanted to bring him back to South Korea with us no matter what.

In the middle of the trip, an argument broke out between me and my mom about this subject. She did not agree with me; she didn't think that we should push things. Above all, she didn't feel comfortable around her son, whom she'd originally been forced to bear against her wishes. She only spoke a little bit of Chinese, and so she had a hard time communicating with him, which complicated their relationship even further.

Furthermore, my mom thought pragmatically; she knew how difficult it would be to bring Chang Qian to South Korea. At first, when we made contact again via telephone once we arrived in Seoul, the farmer had told us that he'd let my brother join us. Now, he was a bit more hesitant.

"One day," he'd say, giving no more details. He was afraid of losing his only son. And he undoubtedly also feared that he would no longer receive money from us in South Korea the day the little boy left to stay with us.

My mother also knew that it would be a huge financial burden if this boy came with us. Being Chinese, my little brother would not be recognized as a defector by the South Korean authorities. After paying a high price for him to get to South Korea with the help of a smuggler, my mom would have to adopt him, the only way for him to legally stay. And of course, he would have no financial aid from the government, which was reserved only for those fleeing from North Korea.

Furthermore, adapting to this ultracompetitive society, for a young Chinese peasant who did not speak a word of Korean, would be nearly insurmountably difficult, particularly in regard to schooling, my mom insisted. However,

I still kept hoping. I told her that it was necessary to bring him back with us, for his future. She didn't listen to me, but I was ready to sacrifice my time and energy to help my brother catch up in school and to teach him good manners. This child was, and still is, very dear to my heart.

During our trip, I tried to speak with him. I had to find some way to convince him to come to Korea of his own volition. If not, his father would be able to accuse us of "kidnapping," and he would be able to take us to court.

But finding a moment to discuss this issue in private proved to be difficult, because the father was wary of us. He was keenly aware of what we were up to and didn't leave his son by himself even for one moment. His father forbade us from sharing the same room, and during the rare moments where I was face-to-face with my brother, he started pouting and changed the topic of conversation. I had the feeling that his father had already told him in advance not to talk about this subject. All my brother did was ask me for more gifts, to buy him this and that, and he always wanted more.

At the end of our vacation, I had failed in my mission. I returned to South Korea with a heavy heart. When would I see my brother again? Would he be even worse off next time? But I refused to give up. Maybe he would mature as he grew up. Maybe he would distance himself from his uncouth father.

Once per month, I still call him from Seoul. He goes to a calling center, in a village not far from the farm, for this long-distance appointment. I try to maintain the relationship, I try to stay positive, and I am determined to help him build a future, no matter what the cost. It's the promise I've made to myself.

❖ 17

On Monday, December 19, 2011, at 7:09 p.m. exactly, right around the time I was finishing this book, I received a text message from a North Korean friend, a refugee like me:

"Kim Jong-il is dead!" the text read.

At the time, I just thought it was a bad joke. These kinds of rumors were frequent around here. But my friend confirmed it. The North Korean news anchor, with tears rolling down her face, had just announced the death of the "Dear Leader." It was true. It was the same woman who had announced the death of Kim Il-sung in 1994. Immediately, I called my boyfriend, the one who had been sent to a labor camp and had suffered so much at the hands of this dictator. Then I called my mom, and I went to meet Keumsun to share this big news. The cruel dictator who had caused so much suffering in our homeland was dead.

"I am so happy to hear that!" my boyfriend told me. But for me, I didn't feel any joy, nor did I feel avenged. There was only one question on my mind: Would the two Koreas finally be reunited?

But I quickly realized that this wasn't going to happen anytime soon. Kim Jong-il's death did not mean the end of the North Korean Kim regime. His third son, Kim Jong-un, was already preparing to take the reins and was ready to do anything to prolong the dictatorship for a third generation. North Korea is the only communist country to have ever been passed down from generation to generation through a hereditary line.

❖

The new dictator Kim Jong-un was only three or four years older that I was, and he was going to decide the future of my country. When I saw him for the first time, I found his chubby face so unsightly that it made me feel a little uncomfortable. However, his youth gave me a sliver of hope. Maybe he would be the one to change the system? Moreover, he had been educated outside the country, in Switzerland. He knew how the rest of the world worked. Maybe this would help guide him in the right direction?

A lot of leading experts expressed their doubts, but I remained hopeful.

In any case, he has no excuse, and no room, for error. Because more and more, North Koreans are getting sick and tired of the regime. More and more of them now know that life is better elsewhere, and that North Korea is nowhere near the "socialist paradise" it claims to be.

❖

On April 15, 2012, the North Korean regime was preparing to celebrate Kim Il-sung's hundredth birthday, the birthday of the "Eternal President." North Korean propaganda had promised the population that the country would become a "rich and powerful" nation by this time. Reading these headlines in the newspaper, I couldn't help but crack a smile, wavering between sadness and anger. When I was young, and when Kim Il-sung was still alive, he had promised us "rice and beef soup" every day. However, more than twenty years later, this simple objective has still not been achieved. I am in a position to judge, because my grandparents and my father died from hunger. And so the promise of a "rich and powerful" nation was a flat-out lie, despite the lavish celebrations orchestrated by the regime.

In reality, all that Kim Jong-un and his family wanted

was to stay in power for as long as possible. They didn't care about the over twenty-two million North Koreans who were wasting away in misery.

However, I believe that the regime will not remain for much longer. Officially, no one can make such predictions with absolute certainty, but information obtained by illegal smugglers along the Chinese border indicates that the North Korean population no longer has as much faith in the regime. Whenever I hear from new defectors from the north, their stories indicate that the disenchantment in the general population is growing stronger and stronger. I find myself thinking that maybe Kim Jong-un will soon find himself face-to-face with a revolution, similar to those during the Arab Spring.

And if that is ever the case, then I will finally be able to go back and visit my hometown, Eundeok. I will see my childhood home again and, most of all, I hope to see my friends from school again. In Seoul, sometimes I daydream about these reunions. I miss my friends so much! In South Korea, everyone regularly sees friends from primary school; it's a social circle that follows you throughout the rest of your life and is always there for you during difficult times. Whenever I see my South Korean friends leave to meet up with their childhood friends, I secretly envy them. It's during these times that I realize that the North Korean regime robbed me of a proper childhood.

But I'm not about to just sit around and spend my days moping. Here in South Korea, I have a future, and I want to be able to give hope to others. Many of my fellow North Koreans have a difficult time adjusting to this ultracompetitive society. They are depressed, because they try their best but don't always succeed at integrating themselves. They feel inferior compared to the native South Koreans. They try to imitate South Koreans, but South Koreans often look at them with disdain. Often, other refugees like me start feeling resentful and fall into depression.

That's why I want to achieve my goals, so that I may one day remind others like myself that there is still hope for them. I want to show my compatriots who have settled down in this country that it is possible to be happy, that it is possible to succeed here. I know that my dreams are ambitious, but I am sincere in them, and I believe I can achieve them. Optimism is a trait that has been deeply ingrained in me. It was passed along to me from my mother, and it is without doubt this sense of positivity that helped us both survive all the hardships we've ever endured, that carried us all the way to our new lives in South Korea.

Epilogue

September 2014

In July 2012, I gazed out the window as my airplane slowed to a stop along the runway. It was already dark outside, but even so I couldn't wait to explore this new country, this country that I had only been able to see in my imagination until this moment. Through the darkness, I could make out rolling fields, the countryside dotted with a few houses. In front of me was the little airport of Springfield, Missouri. So this was it then, the United States? I have to admit, I was slightly disappointed. I had been envisioning tall skyscrapers. Instead, this place looked more like a ghost town.

My long journey to get here began in Seoul. From Seoul, I took a long flight to Chicago, and from there transferred to another flight to reach my final destination of Springfield. At long last, here I was, in the Midwest! Two other students, who had been on the same flight as me, waited with me at the airport. They were from Belarus. The school representatives came to pick us up, and we all climbed into a car. The night was pitch-black. Sleepily, the other students and I rode across the countryside. My stomach grumbled from hunger. After about half an hour on the road, we made a pit stop at a fast-food restaurant along the way, and I ordered a hamburger. I had to pay for the burger myself, which surprised me. In Korea, guests usually aren't expected to pay—the hosts take care of everything. That is our tradition. When we finished eating, we started driving again and continued until we reached the university's campus, our final destination. I found my dorm room and, exhausted by the long journey, I immediately drifted into sleep.

In the morning, my stomach was grumbling again. I decided to leave the safety of my dorm to find something to eat and visit my new environs. However, when I headed out, I was surprised to see that this town was so small, that really it seemed I was in the middle of a field. I walked along the streets and couldn't find a single store. It was so different from Seoul, where little minimarkets lined each street corner. But whenever I crossed paths with people, they greeted me spontaneously with a bright, warm hello. These kind gestures made me smile inside. The people here were so friendly. I was now truly in the United States of America.

❖

My arrival in the United States was the realization of a dream that had formed many months earlier in Seoul. Following the suggestion of a friend of mine, I learned of an online advertisement posted by the American Embassy, which offered scholarships for students to study abroad in America. In South Korea, all students dream of going abroad, especially to the United States. America is the country that Koreans most often aspire to visit, because it's the most powerful country in the world. I myself had also had a desire to travel there, to experience American life for myself and to expand my horizons. Even when I was in North Korea, I found America fascinating. In school as a child, I learned that the United States was our enemy. Americans had blond hair, big noses, and green eyes—or so that's what I was told. For us, the "white" stereotype applied only to Americans—we knew nothing at all of the Europeans' existence. This fascination with the outside world still exists in North Korea: some North Koreans even watch American TV shows in secret. Even though doing so is extremely dangerous, seeing what the outside world is like allows them to dream. In fact, some people who leave North Korea, traveling to Thailand or Laos via China, seek asylum in the United States rather than in South Korea. As for me, when I applied for my scholarship, I wanted to see the United

States, but I also wanted to raise international awareness about the human rights violations still occuring in North Korea.

And that was how I explained it during my interview at the American Embassy. I tried to be as honest as possible while applying for this scholarship, emphasizing the values that I believe in. I did not intend to go to the United States to make money, or to get a job, but to have an experience. I recounted my story, how I had left my homeland due to hunger. I explained that I now had a different kind of hunger: the hunger to see the rest of the world. I wanted to learn how to live with others. The embassy officials asked me a lot of questions. This in fact encouraged me, and I left the appointment with my hopes high. But still I didn't mention the interview to anyone, in case I was disappointed. Studying abroad was, at that point, still just a far-off dream.

One of the requirements was that I had to take the TOEFL, a test of English as a foreign language, a language that I spoke quite poorly. And my fear became a reality: I received an awful score on the exam. To be eligible for the scholarship, a minimum score of 61 was required, but I only received a measly 45. I felt so discouraged. Fortunately for me, the embassy decided to give me another chance, perhaps because my interview had gone so well. I felt encouraged again and studied relentlessly to improve my score.

Finally, a month before the departure date, I was informed that I had been awarded the scholarship. Only three North Korean defectors were selected, and I was one of them. How happy I was! My mom was so proud that she couldn't help but tell every one of her friends, "My daughter is going to America!"

❖

And so that's the story of how, in July 2012, I headed for Missouri, to stay for a year. I was going to improve my English and study psychology, a subject that I am very passionate about. Actually, this was not the first time that I had been to the Western world. A few months earlier, I had had the opportunity to visit another well-known city: Paris! I spent a week there, to present the French edition of the book you now hold in your hands to French journalists and to the French public. I stayed in a small, very old hotel near the Champs-Élysées, the most famous street in the world. My schedule was packed with interviews. The French journalists asked me so many questions. They had never before met a real North Korean, and so they were fascinated, and very kind to me. I was even featured on early-morning TV. We had interviews in cafés, and took photos along the Seine River. It was near the end of winter, and there was still a chilly breeze along the river, but I remained calm in

front of the cameras. To present the book and provide testimony to the human rights situation in North Korea was
my mission, and the purpose of my work.

❖

It was strange to be in that historic city, where the lifestyle
is so urbane and sophisticated, and be talking about famine. I tried to learn as much as I could from the experience.
And of course, let's not forget the French cuisine, which
I had always wanted to taste. At each restaurant that we
went to, I tried a new dish. The first night, I tasted foie
gras, a famous French specialty. I was curious about everything, and even tried saddle of lamb, and of course French
cheese. When someone offered me blue cheese, the first
time I politely accepted but grimaced at the sight. It looked
moldy and smelled very strong. So I carefully took a small
bite ... and, to my surprise, really liked it! So then I tried
it again twice more. Thinking about it, it occurred to me
that cheese is to the French what *kimchi* is to the Koreans.
And the French desserts were so delicious, too. I also did a
bit of tourism, and took a picture in front of the Eiffel Tower.
I like that photo very much. When I returned to Seoul, I
set it as the background picture on my cell phone, as a sou-
venir of that very special week.

❖

In Missouri, the atmosphere was very different, but as the days passed, I found myself more and more charmed by the Midwest, and by the people there. I've often heard that to really get to know America, you have to go out to the countryside, and I believe it. The people there were so polite. They hold the door open for you, which never happens in Korea. This friendliness is one aspect of Western culture that I really appreciate. Of course, there were also less kind people: twice, I was insulted by racist drivers as they drove by. But they were the exception. There, I was able to make friends from all over the world. I discovered that American society is "cosmopolitan" and "mixed." There is no typical "American." One of my friends had a car, and we often went to the neighboring Walmart to shop together. It was the main leisure activity there. I loved seeing all it had to offer, even groceries. I survived a famine as a little girl, after all, so it's only normal that I'm now drawn to food. The prices were much more affordable there than in South Korea, and we often bought supplies to have little parties in the dorms, where we also invited our neighbors. I discovered cuisines from all over the world, as well—for example, Thai food and Arab food. My Saudi friends showed me their specialty: *kapsa*, with rice and chicken. I loved it! During my stay in America, I gained some weight, because I ate so much there.

Everything was so new to me. At the beginning, I shared

a room with a Chinese roommate. It was my first time sharing a room with someone who wasn't part of my family. It
wasn't easy for me at first. She snored, but over time I got
used to it.

Of course, I also did some tourism. I wanted to explore
this big country, even if it was very expensive. I wanted to
go to New York City; it's a city I had always dreamed of
visiting. I often imagined myself drinking a coffee in a café
there. I imagined a very international, sophisticated, luxurious city. But in fact, when I got there, it was a bit different than I had imagined. It was very touristy. The buildings
were packed so closely together that it sometimes made it
feel hard to breathe, almost like I was being suffocated. All
the same, however, that city really is at the center of the
world—I could feel that, and I was thrilled to be there and
experience it. But overall I prefer Chicago, which is much
less condensed. It's a very high-class city.

In terms of my studies, things were much more difficult, and I had to work very hard. For about three months,
I took four hours of English each day to catch up. Then
the "real" psychology classes started, which was a whole new
level of challenge for me, because everything was taught
in English. I did my best to pay attention, but I could often only understand around half of what the professor said.
And every week, I had to write an essay—which was very
difficult for me. I tried my best, but I was only able to get a

C in the class. It was a little discouraging, but I did not let it get me down. I recognized that it was a wonderful opportunity to have had an American classroom experience. I had heard that American students participated a lot more in class than Korean students did, but the difference wasn't too dramatic. In any event, it was the international students who had to work the hardest. But it must also be stated that a lot of American students had part-time jobs to finance their studies. That was something I highly respected, and something South Korean students, who complain so often, could learn from.

For one of my seminar classes, each student had to present his or her native country to the class. So I, of course, spoke of North Korea. I realized that no one in the room really knew much about my native country, but they were curious. Over time, I told them about the challenges I've faced, sharing my life story with them. As a result, a lot of my classmates expressed their respect for me, for having overcome everything that I've experienced. They told me that I had done something extraordinary. My American roommate was particularly fascinated by my story. She knew that I had written a book, but unfortunately, at the time, it was only available in French. She was frustrated about that and so was I. But now here it is in English, right in your hands!

❖

Unfortunately, not everyone is as sympathetic toward North Koreans. South Korean students often distance themselves from me when they find out my origins. It's a sad fact, but it is necessary to point out that in South Korea, the north is still the "enemy." There is always fear of North Korean spies.

As for me, I simply consider myself, above all, Korean. Whenever anyone asks me where I'm from, I respond, "I'm from Korea." And if I'm asked "North or South," I respond, "Both!" I think it's the best answer possible. I want to help the world understand the situation on the Korean peninsula, so that the sufferings of my people are not forgotten. That is why I have chosen to write this book. And to help the world open its eyes to this problem, the ability to speak English is essential.

Thanks to my stay in the United States, my English improved dramatically, even if it is still far from perfect. I returned to Seoul in May 2013, and soon had the chance to test my abilities in English. Over the summer, I received an invitation to London to speak directly to the largest Scandinavian talk show, following the release of this book in Norwegian. I certainly felt nervous. I was to appear next to some big stars, and the host wanted me to speak in English. The producer tested my level in English over the phone. I was hesitant, and a little stressed. Usually, I prefer to speak through an interpreter. But this was an extraordinary chance to tell my story to the public at large. Finally, I accepted, and when the day came, despite my hesitations, I took off for London.

❖

When I landed, the Norwegian producers welcomed me with great warmth. On set, everyone tried to reassure me. The tension was palpable. First it was silent, and then the show began. Some Scandinavian rock stars told how they had risen from humble beginnings to success. Then, the highlight of the night: a large man with green eyes started speaking. I was told he was an English singer who was very famous worldwide. His stage name was Sting.

I had never heard of him—perhaps I was too young, and besides, in North Korea his genre of music is forbidden! When the host asked me whether I knew who Sting was, I admitted that I had had to look up his biography on Google before the show started, so I wouldn't look foolish on camera. The audience laughed. Still, I focused my efforts on telling my story, about my life in Eundeok, where I'm from. At the beginning, I was very nervous about speaking, and my English was halting. But once I got started, I forgot my nervousness, and I told my story for the first time in a foreign language. On the platform, the silence was intense. Everyone listened attentively. I was carried away by emotion when I told the story of my father's death and described his grave, which I have never again been able to visit. I couldn't stop the tears from rolling down my cheeks. When I finished speaking, the crowd applauded. Sting came to talk to me later. He thanked me and we took a photo together. I was deeply moved by how much he and the audience cared. A few weeks later, I learned that the book had become a national best seller in Norway.

After returning from London to Seoul, I finally graduated from Sogang University. But the hard part was only beginning. Now I had to find a job that I liked and that would put my mom, who has not retired despite her old age, at ease. My eventual goal is to become a child psychologist. To achieve that goal, it is my dream to return to the United States for a master's degree. But first, I have to further improve my English and earn another scholarship. Voilà— this is my plan for the next few years.

I undertook the writing of this book with a mission that I hold dear to my heart: providing witness testimony to the situation in North Korea, and helping to alleviate the burdens of my people, who are oppressed by a totalitarian dictatorship. That's why for now, I work for an NGO based in Seoul. The Citizens' Alliance for North Korean Human Rights (NKHR) tries to mobilize world leaders to change the fate of the Korean peninsula north of the 38th parallel, and to help North Korean defectors who have taken refuge in Seoul. With this NGO, I traveled to Jakarta to meet the United Nations special rapporteur on human rights, Marzuki Darusman. This Indonesian diplomat was responsible for preparing a report about the crimes committed by Kim Jong-un's regime. These international efforts have clashed with the inflexibility of the young dictator, who refuses to let UN inspectors within his borders. Nonetheless, I am certain that these international efforts will pay off one day, and that the Kim dynasty will collapse. And when it does, so, too, will the terrible last vestiges of the Cold War.

❖

Now, as I write the last few lines of this book, a memory buried deep in my mind comes back to me. When I was young and living in Eundeok, I remember that on the first floor of our building there lived a young mother. As the famine grew more and more severe, she had a harder and harder time finding food to feed her baby. By the end, she didn't even have enough water to give to the baby. And so one day, famished, the baby died.

That child could easily have been me.

This memory helps me realize how lucky I have been, despite everything, and it gives me the strength to continue pursuing my dreams.

Among my ambitions for the future, there is one that I will never be able to accomplish by myself. It's my dream of one day seeing my people in the north free from a dictatorship that has kept them in fear, misery, and isolation from the rest of the world for decades. For this dream to become a reality, the whole world must open its eyes to the horrors currently taking place in North Korea. The Kim dynasty has so successfully isolated my country that it would be easy for the rest of the world to forget about us. If my memoir can play even a small part in raising global awareness about our suffering and about the tragedies taking place at the hands of this regime, then all that I have endured will not have been in vain.